Raised
on
Fear

Written by Lee Cox & Marge Hulburt

Raised on Fear
Written by Lee Cox and Marge Hulburt
Copyrighted 2004
Published by EVE Foundation
PO Box 828
Milltown, MT 59851
www.endingviolence.net
www.raisedonfear.com

Printed in the U.S.A.

Cover design by Red 440 Design-Kate Likvan, Missoula, MT

All the names and locations in this book have been changed to protect the identities of everyone in my life.

This book is dedicated to all abused children.

The EVE Foundation is funded by the sale of the book "Raised on Fear".

The EVE Foundation is a 501(c)(3) nonprofit organization started in 2005. The programs and projects of the Foundation are committed to stopping domestic abuse.

After you have read this book, please donate it to your local women's shelter, church, local domestic violence program, or give it to a friend.

Thank you for your support.

PO Box 828 Milltown, MT 59851
www.endingviolence.net

Raised on Fear

Welcome

Farewell

Welcome

At 49, life is good. I pull up the covers against the morning chill and listen to my wife's gentle breathing beside me. There is a faint clink and rustle from the kitchen as my daughter finishes breakfast and loads her books for school. With my eyes still closed, I repeat my morning prayer, "God, thank you for helping me."

Before the Beginning

My brother Eddie tells me I was two years old when I wandered under the raised bed of the dump truck my father was repairing. He said the old man freaked out and beat me with the vise grips he was holding in his hand. He said he felt bad that he could not protect me or stop me from being hit by our father. He was seven years old.

I grew up in a world of violence and unpredictability. I learned to protect myself the best I could. I learned to take care of myself because no one else would. I learned to lie, to conceal, and to cover my fear with anger and violence.

It has been a twenty-year journey for me to find the place where there is love for me, where I can release the fear that comes so easily to me and let anger melt. I have found forgiveness for my father who was so brutal and for my mom who was unable to help me or herself. I have found peace within myself and meaning in my life.

No one knew the abuse that went on in our home, as we all learned to keep it hidden. No one knew my wish to make it stop. And later, no one knew the fear that overwhelmed me and drove me to hit and hurt the ones I loved most.

This is the story of my life. I have found a way out of my anger and fear. Others can, too. By telling my story, it is my wish to bring hope of healing to others who have been abused. It is my wish to give those who are in an abusive family the strength to

1

get out and get help for themselves and their loved ones. And it is my wish to awaken anyone who will listen to the responsibility we all have to speak for those who do not have a voice.

I asked my mom about Eddie's story, and she said it was true. She said my father had beaten me for walking under the truck to insure it would never happen again. It wasn't his fault, she said; his brother had died from a car falling on him. She couldn't stop him, she said; she was too afraid.

For most of my life, I felt that I was followed by a curse. Things went wrong for me, and no matter how hard I tried, somehow I was always screwed out of the things I wanted most. I got the curse from my father who got it from his mom. Some say the curse has been in our family for generations. Others say it began on a sunny autumn day in a northwest Oregon logging camp. The year was 1929.

With the camp equipment in good repair, Grandpa Cox was taking advantage of the quiet afternoon to work on the family car. He took my Uncle Daniel, three years old, by the hand, and the two of them sauntered outside to give Grandma room to prepare the logging crew's evening meal.

It was a routine brake job. Grandpa handed Daniel a toy dump truck and sat him in a pile of soft dirt by the car. He gathered his tools and laid them neatly on a piece of canvas. He got out the bumper jack, raised the front end of the car, and smiled at Daniel playing happily by himself.

He removed both front wheels and used a small hammer to dislodge the bearings. Setting them on the canvas, he removed the worn brake linings. He worked with precision and accuracy as he carefully replaced the old linings with new ones.

Picking up the bearings, he headed for the camp workshop to clean and repack them with new grease. "Anything worth doing is worth doing right" was his motto. The car would be better than new when he was done.

Clean parts in hand, he made his way back to the car. As he rounded the corner of the house, he stopped. The car lay silently on its front bumper, the jack lying in the dirt, and Daniel pinned, lifeless, beneath the car.

I am told that Grandma never forgave Grandpa for Daniel's death, and she spent her life as an angry and bitter woman. She raised six children in anger, and in 37 years of marriage, she and Grandpa never felt relief from the "curse."

My father, Donald Edward, was just a year old when Daniel died and often felt the brunt of Grandma's anger. I do not believe that Grandma was ever sorry for anything she did out of anger. She did not grieve anything. I know that in all that happened in our family, my father never grieved anything, either, or ever said he was sorry. He was never sorry for anything he did that hurt anyone. Behind the family anger was tremendous fear, fear of grief, guilt, and the unknown.

I was born into a family of anger and had no choice but to live with it. I believe my father had no choice, and neither did my grandma, and perhaps neither did countless generations before her. My grandma's reaction to her pain affected her husband, her children, and her grandchildren. It infected generations of people who have no idea they carry the poison created by her response to her pain. I do not believe she knew; it is just the way things were. And I do not believe it started with her. But it can end with me. Perhaps it has always been my mission to end violence everywhere.

When I look at my father's life I see my own. I see the path my life could have followed and did indeed follow for more years than I care to remember. When I finally learned that I could become the creator of my life and change my life experience, I had not only triumphed over my own struggles but over those of my father and generations of my family before him.

I was born to worship a man who taught me I was a victim and that my life was worthless. Those imprints will be with me for the rest of my life. I know they are untrue, and yet they affect me in everything I do. I accept that they are there and have learned to live my life as a loving and creative force. My father was unable to do that and is living out his life as a victim, struggling in anger against forces he doesn't understand and can't control.

Tragedy befell my father when he was thirteen and confirmed the existence of the family curse. My father, Don, was the oldest of four children at that time, and my Uncle Harold, age four, was the youngest. Their mother had just returned from a trip to the grocery store, and hearing the car pull in, Don immediately went out to help unload the groceries. Harold was at his heels. Their mother was already unloading the first two bags. As she backed away from the car, Harold scrambled into the driver's seat. He bounced on the seat, grinning. He honked the horn and turned the wheel from side to side, making engine sounds with his voice. Just as Don reached in for a bag of groceries Harold stepped on the clutch. The car rolled forward and forced the door closed on Don's hips. The curse was back.

At first, it appeared to be nothing more than a bad bruise, but over the next few weeks Don's right hip refused to heal. When two months had passed, his father finally insisted that his mother take him to see a doctor.

After a battery of tests, the doctor was unapologetic. "I'm afraid your son has a condition called osteomyelitis," he said. "It's an infection that causes deterioration of the bones. In your son's case, it has infected his hip and will spread throughout his body with time." He recommended immediate hospitalization in order to save Don's life.

On the drive home, the only words from his mother were, "Damn car." And Harold has never forgiven himself for ruining Don's life.

Don spent three years in Good Samaritan Hospital in Portland. He was given a room with two beds, but the second bed was rarely used. He entertained the hospital staff, and often they could be found congregated in his room during their off hours.

He always had a book in his hand and loved reading from the encyclopedia. With the help of a tutor, he finished high school and two years of college while he was there, all before his 16th birthday. People who knew him at the time say he was charming and highly disciplined. He impressed everyone with his uncanny talent for numbers, being likened to a human calculator.

He met a judge during his stay who had just lost a son to World War II. The judge immediately took a liking to him, and when he learned Don was interested in studying medicine or law, he offered to pay all expenses for any school Don chose to attend.

His parents sold nearly everything they owned to pay the hospital bills. They had been told in no uncertain terms that they had to pay or take their son home. His mother's anger gave her the strength to work two jobs and visit her son every day. She was never known to take a day off, ever. They could only afford one car, which his father drove to work, and his mother walked to work and climbed the hill to the hospital every single day. Don's eight-year-old sister, Alice, sold her clarinet to help with the bills.

Don was plagued by the fact that the only cure for his disease was amputation, and he was constantly at odds with the doctors over this, trying to protect his deteriorating leg.

Shortly after his 16th birthday, his attention was caught by a familiar voice. It was one of the doctors speaking. "We have no choice but to remove the leg," he said. "The infection is spreading, and it's going to take his life."

In the silence, he heard his mother speak. "What will it cost?" she said.

Immediately, Don began planning his escape. Despite his withered leg, he moved expertly on crutches. He charmed a friend's wife, who was a nurse at the hospital, into taking an adventure with him to New Orleans. There he quickly found work in a packaged liquor store. He bought Wellington boots and had a three-inch lift made for his right foot. He taught himself to walk without crutches, although he could never completely rid himself of the limp.

The nurse soon returned to Portland saying the adventure was nothing like Don had said it would be.

Within just a few months, Don met and married Catherine, nine years his senior, and eagerly settled into his role as husband and father to her two children.

He never returned to Portland and never contacted the judge. When asked in later years why he did not go back to school, he would say, "I like my life just the way it is."

His father never stopped looking for Don. He hired private detectives in Portland to help with the search, but to no avail. The family eventually moved to Deer Park, Washington. Two years after Don's disappearance, a letter arrived in the mail. Don had been found.

His father immediately called the liquor store and asked to speak to Don. There was silence as the phone changed hands, then Don said hello.

"Son," said his father, "This is your dad. How are you doing?"

Don and Catherine soon came home to visit, but it was only a matter of days before the curse raised its ugly head. Don's osteomyelitis recurred in full force, and he was rushed to the local hospital. He was soon transferred to a larger hospital in Spokane, just over a hundred miles away.

In his absence, his mother and Catherine became quick friends, and while Don was still in the hospital, Catherine returned unexpectedly to New Orleans. It was only a matter of weeks before Father received divorce papers and no explanation. He was certain his mother had driven Catherine away.

He was discharged from the hospital broke and disillusioned, but his anger couldn't hide the fact that his family needed him. His brother Harold and three sisters were still at home, and his father had aged tremendously over the two years he'd been away. He stayed as his family lost their café and turned to sharecropping. He threw his energy into farming and stayed as they lost most of the crops to bad weather that year. He helped load the family possessions into a large storage van and move the family in with his mother's brother.

His parents found work, and Don took a job in construction on the Grand Cooley Dam. He pushed himself to work long hours and saved the lion's share of his earnings for a house for his folks. Even with his bad leg, he could outwork any two men.

He had developed huge muscles in his arms and good leg, and he was smart and ambitious.

He even stayed after his father called one night to tell him the storage van had burned up with all their things inside. He redoubled his efforts, and eventually his parents were able to purchase a small house.

With the curse temporarily at bay, Don quit his job and moved to Moses Lake. He craved the warmth and stability of a family of his own. The first ingredient was a stable job, and he set his sights on the Bureau of Reclamation. He had made up his mind to work there, and so he did.

It was at the Bureau that Dad met my mom, Ella Robb, and in three weeks he had made her his wife.

Ella was a tall, good-looking gal who loved horses and had many friends. Despite all evidence, she saw herself as isolated, fat, and ugly. At thirteen, her mother sent her to see a psychologist because she seemed so unhappy. "I didn't tell him anything," Ella later said, "and eventually I didn't have to go back."

At 18, she married. When she became pregnant six months later, her new husband immediately left her. She moved back home with her parents and gave birth there to my brother Eddie Allan. At her parents' suggestion, she left Eddie with them and moved in with her Aunt Clara, near Portland, to attend business school.

Upon graduation, she quickly found work in the dime store in Moses Lake. Living at home, she was able to work while her folks took care of Eddie. She rapidly progressed to working for a lawyer's office, then a bank, and then, through her father's influence, for the Bureau of Reclamation. As part of the secretarial pool at the Bureau, she earned more than she had ever thought possible and looked forward to being able to afford a place of her own.

It was her father who introduced her to Don. What it was about Don that especially attracted her, she was never quite sure. He was charming, convincing, and very presentable. His voice, posture, and presence were commanding. He was attractive and persistent in his pursuit.

Their marriage, in April of 1951, changed the lives of everyone in the family.

Father and Mom settled comfortably into a little trailer provided by the Bureau. Husband, wife, and son. Eddie had a father, and things were as they should be.

The first thing Mom noticed about Father was that he never did laundry. He had closets full of dirty clothes. When things got too dirty, he stuffed them into cupboards and bought new ones. Father included Eddie in everything they did together. He seemed overly strict, but at least Eddie had a father now. That was enough for Mom to overlook what she later called Father's "mean streak."

Father was stricter with Eddie than Grandpa Robb had been. When Eddie got out of line, Father would whack him on the butt, grab him, and shake him. Father's rules were absolute, with no tolerance for mistakes, and the consequences were always extreme for the situation. Grandpa spoke to Father one time about how strict he was with Eddie, and Father told him to stick to his own business. Grandpa never interfered again.

It wasn't long after they were married that Father hit Mom, as well. They were talking in bed one night, and the conversation gradually became a disagreement, then an argument, and then he hit her. "There was no real damage," she says, "I didn't get a black eye." She doesn't even remember the conversation.

She thought of leaving him in those early years, but thought, "How stupid could a person be to have been married twice at my age," and she stayed. She stayed because of not wanting to look stupid.

During their first anniversary celebration Mom announced she was pregnant. With the promise of a larger family, Father went to work immediately on their future. He made arrangements to purchase a couple acres of land just outside the city limits. He made a deal on a contract that would allow him to build the house and pay for the lot when the house was finished and he got his mortgage.

Father worked all day for the Bureau and late into the night, every night, building his dream home. There were two neighbors also building homes close to his.

Despite all his efforts, by July Father was behind schedule and needed to complete the house to obtain a loan. He quit the Bureau in late July and worked on the house full time through November. Mom had quit working as well because of the pregnancy. They gave up their home and moved into the new, unfinished house. Eddie stayed with his grandparents a few miles away.

No matter how hard Father tried, one thing after another seemed to interfere with the completion of the house. There was no city water available because they were outside the city limits. Halfway through the project, Father determined it would be a duplex instead of a single-family home. The banks would not talk about financing an unfinished home to an unemployed couple.

As smart as he was, my father never did his homework. He pretended that he knew everything, and he was very convincing, even to himself.

In November, with no heat or water, they rented a room at a motel. Mom would stay with Father at the house while he worked late into the evening. Then they would go to the motel to sleep. This continued until November 24, when Dallas Edward was born.

Mom was in the hospital for three days, during which time Father borrowed his in-laws' camper trailer and set it up in a small trailer court next to the hospital. It had no bathroom, there was just the public shower and bath in the trailer court, but it was warm and affordable. He had it all set up for Mom and Dallas when they got out of the hospital. He continued to work on the house full time, trying to get it done before the contract deadline.

On December 3, the contract called for payment in full. On December 4, Father lost the house. He blamed everyone except himself, and he was angry at everyone for his loss.

It was winter, and work was not easy for Father to find. As Mom would recall, losing the house brought out a side to Father that she had never seen, but always suspected. He could get very angry and be very mean. It came out at the strangest times. He was much more critical of how meals were cooked and how his laundry was done. Mom was on heightened alert to do things "right."

All winter Father struggled for work. His lawyer managed to collect $2,700 on the house deal, but after attorney's fees, Father did not end up with enough to cover what he had spent on materials.

Valentine's Day came with a temperature of 3 degrees and the air dancing with crystals of snow. Mom and Father spent a quiet, lazy morning at home and the afternoon visiting with their best friends, Marge and Harry. It was a short drive home, and Mom fixed a simple dinner. They settled the boys into bed and grabbed a book to read before going to sleep.

It was almost 10:00 pm when Dallas awoke crying. Father walked down the hall and comforted the baby. It wasn't long before he was sleeping again, and Father went back to bed. A half hour later, the baby awoke again, and again Father comforted him back to sleep.

Around midnight, Father awoke and got up to check on Dallas. He found that Dallas had kicked off his covers. As he pulled the covers over the baby's body, he could sense that something was wrong. He shook the baby gently and realized that Dallas was not breathing. He picked up the baby and yelled to Mom to meet him at the hospital.

With baby Dallas in his arms, he ran on his crippled leg across the frozen field separating the trailer court from the hospital. He didn't feel the rocks or icy weeds against his bare feet.

There was nothing the doctors could do. They called it crib death.

Grandma Cox made all the arrangements for the funeral. During the service, it was with shock and horror that the family heard the minister say that Dallas Edward would not be allowed in heaven because he had not been baptized. Mom watched in silence as they lowered the small coffin into the cold, frozen ground.

With Father out of work, the burial expenses were more than they could afford. A white wooden cross marked the spot where they had buried their son. Weeks later, Mr. Morris, the mortician, provided free-of-charge a small, concrete headstone with the word "Cox" on the cold, flat surface. When Mom arrived at the cemetery, she was astounded to find that Mr. Morris had placed it on the wrong grave. She expressed her concern, but it was never moved and she withdrew.

There was no time to grieve. She took a job as a waitress in Elmer's Chinese American Restaurant. She shuddered any time she saw anybody with a baby and for months tried to avoid looking at babies at all.

Through the help of Grandpa Robb, Father landed a position with Stillwell Engineering as part of a surveying crew for Larsen Air Force Base in Moses Lake. With the new employment, they swiftly moved from the little camper into a rental house.

It wasn't long before Father came home with the news that his company would be relocating. They were government contractors, and when this contract was complete, they would move on. Mom was clear she was not moving.

Grandpa Robb told Father of an opening on the air base, driving truck. With this job came the opportunity for government housing, and the family moved into a duplex in the government section of town.

In the Beginning

I believe that I became a part of my family at conception. It was only a month or two after Dallas' death that my mom discovered she was pregnant with me, and I like to imagine I brought some measure of comfort into her life. Having just moved, and with Father and Mom both working, there was new hope in the air.

After just a few weeks Mom quit her job in the restaurant, saying the work was just too much with being pregnant. She stayed home, as her mother had done, cooking, cleaning, and taking care of Father and Eddie. Father soon moved up in his company and was delivering cement.

Whenever he was in the neighborhood, Father would stop by the house, pick up Eddie, and take him along in the truck. In the evenings, Father would carefully leave his lunchbox where Eddie could find it. Eddie would approach the lunchbox with a gleam in his eye. "Will it be in there?" he'd think. He'd flip the clasp and open the lid. Without fail, there would be a sucker in there for him to find. Mom would smile whenever she saw these hints of joy and bonding between father and son.

Eddie did not share Mom's bliss. He was angry at her for bringing this man into their lives, a man who was strict and controlling and who had to be watched and obeyed. To this day, he is angry at Mom and hides his true feelings, pretending to be nice to her. For her part, Mom says, "In a way, I am as guilty as their father was, for not doing anything to stop the violence. I am lucky my children speak to me. At least they are kind to my face."

Mom's home life came at a price. She was not a good cook, according to Father, and a terrible housekeeper in his eyes. She was a "shit stacker." She would have stacks of things in all the corners. Father would spend hours telling her how to cook. He knew everything about cooking, and everything else. Nothing Mom did was "right" enough for Father, and she lived in constant fear of doing things wrong. The smallest things would set Father off, and he did not hesitate to hit her or Eddie or both of them. Doing things wrong was the most feared thing in our house because the wrath of Father could be unbearable.

When he wasn't hitting Mom, he was threatening her. He threatened to kill her. He threatened to make her so ugly no one would want her. He threatened never to let her see her children again. He threatened to come and get her if she left.

In front of other people, Father was always a really nice guy. He always put on a good face. He loved socializing and playing cards with the neighbors, all the while devising ways to win by cheating and sending signals to Mom. At home, he looked for reasons to justify his anger, always looking for what was wrong and never praising anyone inside the family. Mom screwed up everything: the cooking, the cheating at cards, the housecleaning. There was a constant feeling of "being in trouble" in our family. Mom learned early in the marriage that staying out of trouble was the smart thing to do. Even today, she says, "Some of the violence was my fault. I made it worse by talking back or nagging." The best thing to do was to go along.

When asked if there was anything she loved about Father, she replied, "There must have been. I was with him for 36 years."

But I have never heard her say anything about love or loving him. At first she was ashamed to leave, then she was trapped and afraid. When he eventually left her for another woman, his divorce was the biggest favor in the world. He never would have stopped abusing her. He never would have changed. He never would have changed with her.

I was born on Dec. 9, 1953. Mom tells me the thing she remembers about my birth was a lady named Leotta who gave birth to a baby boy on the same day. The only difference was that Leotta gave her son up for adoption. Mom says that she didn't "feel" anything about me. Perhaps she wasn't ready for another child, or perhaps she was afraid to love me.

When I ask her about my early childhood, her answer is always the same, "You were a good boy." Her decisions about me were based on how my father responded to me. Father held his distance.

The first year of my life was spent traveling to and from the doctor's office. My parents were so afraid I would die. When Dallas died, my parents did not really have an answer for what had happened. They second guessed themselves and did not want another baby to die. I spent most of my time quietly in a crib or playpen, but at the first whimper or runny nose I was taken to Doctor Tracey. My experience was that of being held at arm's length. I have no sense of ever being held or cuddled by my mom or my father. Everyone was scared to touch me, afraid that I would die.

Moses Lake was in an economic boom at that time, with the building of Larsen Air Force Base to house the Titan missiles. Dad hooked up with a neighbor, George Berg, who had an inside track on contracting with the air base for hauling. He and Father bought three used dump trucks, Father borrowing his half of the money from Grandpa Cox, and they were soon operating a profitable business.

Eighteen months later, the government had completed the material hauling portion of the job, and George and Father were out of work. "Don," George suggested, "Why don't we relocate and keep the business going? There are plenty of opportunities outside Moses Lake." Father smiled. He and George made a good team.

He brought up the idea with Mom, and they talked. But again, Mom was very clear that she did not want to move. She was not moving. Period.

Father and George split up the equipment, leaving Father with two of the trucks. He repaid Grandpa Cox and watched as George and his wife drove off for California.

With the contract over, we moved out of government housing and rented the top floor of an old farmhouse. Father had trouble finding work for the dump trucks, being cursed with one problem after another, and Mom was pregnant again.

Father continued to take Eddie with him in the truck. One day he decided that Eddie could drive the dump truck ahead while he loaded dirt and gravel from the side of the road. He gave Eddie instructions and placed him behind the wheel. He put the truck in granny gear, and it slowly moved forward. All Eddie had to do was steer. This was too much for a boy of seven, and Eddie couldn't keep the truck going straight. Soon, Father threw down his shovel and pulled Eddie from the truck. He struck Eddie about the head and shoulders, yelling at him all the while.

As Eddie would later recall, "He yanked me out of the truck, beat the crap out of me, and put me back behind the wheel, telling me I'd better get it right." To this day, Eddie hates big trucks.

Eddie had such a hard time with Father that he did not remember anything about our childhood when I first asked him. This is a family trait, forgetting what's happened. We do not remember things that don't feel good; nobody in the family does.

Father soon sold one of the trucks. It was a severely cold winter, and Mom recalls huddling around an oil stove trying to keep warm. Father struggled to find work. Before winter was over, he sold the second truck to keep food on the table.

Grandma Cox and Uncle Daryl sewed and converted Father's clothes into a wardrobe fit for a car salesman. Father took a job selling cars for the Oldsmobile dealership, and soon things were looking up. He got to drive new cars home every day, and he always came home bragging about how good he had done that day. Once again, he was earning the money he needed to support his growing family.

In March, my younger brother Albert Dallas arrived. As the nurse brought him to my mom's side, Father's eyes lit up, and he exclaimed, "What a beautiful baby!" At that moment, Mom knew Albert was special and he would be her favorite.

My world was changing. I had been the baby of the house for 2-1/2 years. My parents had paid attention to everything about me. They had taken me to the doctor's office all the time. Now all the attention was on the new boy.

It was more than simple sibling rivalry. They treated Albert differently. My mom loved holding him. Every day I watched the way she treated him. I can still feel anger well up inside my throat just thinking about the way Mom treated him.

It was not long after Albert arrived that Mom was back to spending her days riding horses, sewing, and cooking. She seemed happier since Albert had come into the world.

This was the beginning of my war with Albert. He was the enemy, and I hated him.

The following spring, when I was 3-1/2, Grandpa Robb was transferred out of the area, and Mom and Father bought my grandparents' house in Cascade Valley. It was a modest, two-bedroom home which Grandpa had built himself, with a small, two-car garage. It was on a double lot backed by a large field belonging to a neighboring farm. To me it was a mansion with a huge yard, the biggest in the neighborhood.

Father had plans for making the house right. He did not approve of the way Grandpa Robb had built it.

Eddie, Albert, and I shared a bedroom. Father sold cars. Mom took care of the house, the cooking, and Albert. She was pregnant again, and I was aware of more competition for my mom's attention.

Father's attention was not something anyone wanted. It was as though he carried a gun of anger. When it was holstered, life was fairly predictable, but when he took it out, you never knew who or what was going to get it. Most of the time, the "look" was enough to stop anything that irritated Father. But when his tongue went over his lower teeth, that was the sure sign someone was about to get hurt.

Each of us has our stories about experiencing the wrath of Father. Eddie caught the worst of it. Father seemed bound and determined to teach Eddie how to be. My way of dealing with it was to disappear. I spent my time hiding out and not being noticed.

I used to follow Eddie around like a pet puppy. He was so cool in my eyes. He was smart, tall, and had lots of friends. Sometimes I would not be allowed to go with him, but when I was... oh, the polliwog pond, the tree climbing, hiding in the farmer's fields, and most importantly, going to the little store for treats. Life did not get any better than when I was with Eddie.

School started, and Eddie was off to first grade. I was so jealous that he got to spend time away from home. He got all those fancy new clothes and he rode that big, yellow bus. How I dreamed of the day I would be on that bus with him.

It was about this time that Grandpa Robb died. He loved fishing, and it was on the Smith River near Great Falls, Montana that he passed away. He, Grandma, and another couple had been fishing since early morning. Feeling very tired, and with his arm hurting, he lay down beside the bank of the river and drifted off to sleep. It was his heart. He died quickly, without pain, doing what he loved most in his life, fishing.

Father moved Grandma Robb to our neighborhood, a block from our home. I couldn't wait to visit her. I remembered all the times I'd spent with Grandma and Grandpa before they moved away. When I would visit, Grandma used to sit on my bed and read stories to me while Grandpa snored. Boy, could he snore! I also remembered the drawer in her kitchen where she kept the suckers. It was a white, metal kitchen cabinet, and the suckers were in the third drawer down.

Soon, the hateful day came when Jenny was born. She arrived home in a beautiful white basket. She was small and dressed in a pink blanket and frilly white outfit. My father called her "his little princess."

Her presence in the house gave me feelings of being worthless, alone, and unimportant. She was the final evidence I needed to prove I was in the wrong family, maybe on the wrong planet. There was no thinking about it; that was just the way it was. I was all I had, and that was just the way it was.

Eddie, Albert, and I slept in the second bedroom of the house Grandpa had built. It was only a few days after Jenny's arrival when Father announced the beginning of the remodeling project we had heard so much about. He would remodel the second bedroom for Albert and Jenny. Eddie and I were moved to the utility room on the back of the house. He put in a makeshift closet and a dresser along with our bunk bed, and we were set.

Father had always complained about the way Grandpa had built the house, so the remodel was just the thing to make the house right. He did the living room, the two regular bedrooms, the bathroom, and the dining room. He installed electric heat in the ceilings, hand plastered all the walls and ceilings, and created a beautiful home. Our room he didn't touch. It always felt to me like a place where you put things you do not want.

One afternoon, after Father and his friend Lou had finished plastering the walls in Albert and Jenny's bedroom, I snuck in and looked around. It was the most beautiful pink I had ever seen, bright and alive with color. It was perfect. The plaster was still soft, and with my finger on the wall where Albert's bed would be, I carved the letters, A-L-B-E-R-T. That would do it. The old man would get him now.

Albert, of course, was not even a suspect in the crime. I was immediately accused of doing the carving, which I obstinately denied. What surprised me was that Father seemed to be confused by my denial. He couldn't make sense of why I would carve Albert's name into the wall, then stand and lie in the face of being caught.

I was never clear on the punishment. Yep, I got a whipping, but was it for the lying, the carving, or for being stupid? I settled on for being stupid. Boy, was I stupid!

There were different levels of punishment in my world. The whack could be applied to any part of the body with an open hand. Then there was the pants up belt whipping, then the pants down, bare butt, grabbing the ankles. So as to define each and give them a name: whack – bare hand on anything, spanking – pants on with belt, whipping – pants down with belt, beating – total annihilation by any means available or necessary.

Before receiving punishment, Father always gave the same speech, "This is going to hurt me more than you, but I have to get your attention." Then at the end, he would say, "Now that I have your attention," blah, blah, blah...

Some other favorite sayings were: "I am going to whip you 'til your boots are filled with blood," "Jesus H. Christ, what the hell is wrong with you?" "You're just too stupid to learn," "You are as dumb as a box of rocks," and, "I brought you into this world, I can take you out."

Jenny was six months old when Father decided he had had enough of being a father and husband. It was never clear what was the final straw, the house being dirty, dinner not cooked right or on time, or the lack of appreciation for all that he gave us. He came home from work and started breaking dishes, tipping over furniture, and yelling about what animals we were and how we did not deserve anything. He had done everything for us and gotten nothing in return.

It was not long before he had packed his suitcase and left, vowing never to return. Mom never shed a tear. "Fine," was her only comment.

Grandma came over to watch us right away, while Mom went off to look for a job. She was hired immediately to work mornings at the coffee bar in Ditzens Grocery. Grandma watched us while Mom worked, and a peacefulness settled over our household.

In four days, Father was back. There was no explanation, no apology; he was just back, as though nothing had ever happened. We would later learn that he had traveled to Seattle and landed a job there working in a car lot. It only lasted one day, and he returned home. It was never talked about. He was finished selling cars.

Father had accumulated a small savings account and got the idea to start a business building and repairing boats. With Mom working, there was enough income to meet the essentials for the family, so Father worked on boats at home.

Mom soon had the opportunity to return to Elmer's Chinese American Restaurant, working the evening shift. The pay was better, but she was now away from home five nights a week.

Mom pre-cooked all our dinners, and even though Father complained about her cooking, he warmed them. He loved commanding the house in her absence. As long as we did exactly what we were told, trouble was avoided.

Doing dishes was always an issue. At first we were too slow. Then Father trained us to get them done in twenty minutes or get a whipping. It only took a couple of whippings before Eddie and I could complete the dishes in less than twenty minutes every time.

Occasionally, there were late-night dish inspections. Our bedroom was beside and behind the kitchen. Being able to listen to what Father was doing in the kitchen created the illusion of being prepared for whatever might come.

It would start with his walk being slower, heavier, and more pronounced than usual. In the kitchen, we could hear the dishes being set on the counter. At this point, my mind wants to go blank, but I can remember listening to him walk into our doorway and say coldly, "I want to see you boys in the kitchen right now."

There was nowhere to go. It was a long walk from my bed to the door, maybe five feet. I rounded the corner and saw the cupboard completely emptied. "I told you boys what would happen if I found dirty dishes one more time."

I thought about how wrong this was. It wasn't my fault. I didn't know who had done those dishes, but I didn't think we had done them.

Whatever it was I said then was wrong. Father exploded. So after a good, strong whipping with the belt, there were all those dishes to do and twenty minutes to get them done.

Over the next three years, dish inspections happened a couple times a year. We would usually be woken up at night by being grabbed by the ankle and pulled out of bed onto the floor. From the age of five, I never really slept.

This is when I began to get an inkling that something in our family was seriously wrong. I could find no one else who had dish inspections in the middle of the night, and it made no sense because he would inspect dishes we had not used in months.

In the fall of 1958, I started school, and Grandma Robb moved in next door! Father decided to fix a place for Grandma's trailer next to our house. He put in an additional septic tank and dug a ditch from the well house to the trailer. He added a 10' X 30' covered patio in the front.

Father had a reverence for Grandma. He took great care of her and always treated her with respect and kindness. She was a huge part of our lives. She was loving and accepting of everyone, even Father. She loved me and treated me as though I were special. She always believed in me. She taught me to pray, and her house was a safe port in the constant storm of my life. Living next door, she immediately started giving each of us piano lessons.

My father did a lot of mean and nasty things to our family, but he always made sure Grandma was taken care of.

Boyhood in Moses Lake

My first thought about kindergarten was, "School, what an incredible invention!" The teacher, Miss Cooper, was gentle, kind, and caring. There were pads to lie on during naptime, and there were snacks. I decided right away that this was someone I wanted to impress. On the third day of school, I took an apple as a gift for her. That worked so well that it was only a few days before I was appointed to pass out the snacks.

Snacks were kept on a shelf in the coat area. It was the same thing every day. Someone would pass out the cookies while Miss Cooper poured the milk. It was a great honor to pass out cookies. I quickly realized that there were always extra cookies, and as I passed them out, I would treat myself to an extra helping every now and then. It was pure heaven. Grandma always spoke of heaven on earth... Well, passing out cookies was as close to this as I believed anyone had ever been.

One beautiful fall afternoon, Mom was home from work, and the family project was shelling walnuts. We cracked open the shells and placed the nuts in plastic containers. I was easily bored with cracking shells and kept myself busy daydreaming. "What a great gift these walnuts would make for my teacher," I thought.

I asked my mom if I could take a container to Miss Cooper. She thought it was a great idea. I rode the bus in the mornings, and Mom picked me up every day about noon. So off I went to school on Monday morning, my box of walnuts in hand. I set them on Miss Cooper's desk and said, "These are for you."

Miss Cooper looked at me and said, "Well, how much are they?"

There was no hesitation in my voice. "Fifty cents," I said. The response was easy and obvious.

Miss Cooper said, "I'll pay your mom when she picks you up."

"Sure," I said, and that was the end of it. Or so I thought.

Mom arrived at her normal time to pick me up, and Miss Cooper walked me to the car. As I got in, Miss Cooper walked around to the driver's side and handed Mom the fifty cents. She and Mom exchanged a few words, and Mom made her keep the fifty cents and was very apologetic.

As we drove away, I was confused by Mom's anger. I thought I had just done something great. I had made a deal, the first real deal of my life. I had made money, and I had gotten something from giving. Wasn't that one of the goals in life? Mom just spoke of how embarrassed she was. She kept explaining to me how wrong it was. If it was wrong, why did it feel so good?

I felt anger at the thought I might be wrong. I decided that Mom was wrong, not me. I put her on my list of people who could not be trusted.

That summer, Father's brother, Uncle Harold, came to visit. I saw him sitting in Father's chair one afternoon and climbed up into his lap. I asked him what time it was, and he explained that it was time for me to learn to tell time.

I did not want to learn to tell time, I just wanted to know what time it was. For the next thirty minutes, Uncle Harold focused on me and teaching me to tell time. It wasn't what I wanted to do, but the kind and gentle way he taught me was incredible, and I learned to tell time. I also learned that he was someone I could trust; he would not hurt me.

In first grade, I learned to write in cursive. I practiced and practiced writing the name "Don." Since my birth, I had been called by my middle name, "Lee," because my parents had thought it would be too confusing to have two "Don's" in the house. Now I wanted to be "Don," strong and commanding like my father, worthy in his eyes.

One Saturday afternoon, I spotted Father sitting in his favorite chair. I grabbed a sheet of paper from my bedroom and picked up an ink pen off the table. I strode into the living room and knelt at the coffee table. I laid out my paper on the table and beautifully scripted the letters D-O-N.

I jumped to my feet and proudly walked across the room, interrupting Father's conversation with Mom. I handed him my accomplishment. He looked at the letters on the paper, then quickly looked at the table, and I could see by his face that something was wrong.

"Look at what you've done," he commanded. I was lost as he grabbed my arm and escorted me to the end of the coffee table where I had been writing. "You've ruined my coffee table." His words filled the air like an explosion. Listening to how stupid I was, was more than I could hear. All the statements about how children ruined everything decent he owned were enough for me to know that I was truly stupid and cursed with bad luck. I made a decision at that moment that I would be smarter in the future; I would always figure out what I was doing before I did anything.

I remember being six years old and sitting at the dinner table. It was a small table in the kitchen, pushed against one wall.

My father was cooking zucchini for dinner, dipped in egg batter and fried in grease. It was one of his favorite dishes, but to me the smell that filled the kitchen was revolting. When my father finished cooking, he came over and sat down at the table. I had two pieces of zucchini on my plate, and I was totally avoiding them. There were mashed potatoes, meatloaf, and the zucchini. I had eaten everything else, but Father ordered me to clean my plate. I hesitated and watched his tongue roll over his lower teeth. I knew I was in trouble. "You will eat that," he said, "or I will take off my belt and give you a whipping."

I looked at him and at the zucchini on my plate. I reached down with my fork and picked up the first one. As I quickly stuffed it into my mouth, I knew it would not stay down. The smell alone was almost enough to make me vomit, and the feeling in my mouth of the slimy, greasy, green stuff was the final straw. I knew I couldn't eat it, and I wasn't going to eat it, no matter what he did. As I vomited up all my dinner on the table, I realized the power I had to stop anyone from making me do anything I really did not want to do. I did not get whipped, and in my own way I had won, and I knew it.

This was my first huge act of resistance. It was a turning point in my life. I knew then I had power to protect myself from anything, absolutely anything, even the curse.

After three years of working the swing shift, Mom started working mornings. The change was hard to deal with. Mom was a morning person, up early, and cheery and happy for the most part. Then all of a sudden we were at the mercy of Father and his ways. There was no place to hide from him in the morning.

Father's method of waking Eddie and me up was to come in, grab us by the ankle, pull us out of bed, and drop us on the floor. I slept on the bottom bunk and could normally awaken and get my feet on the floor before Father was finished yanking Eddie out of bed. I learned to always sleep with one eye open.

Life was a set of contradictions. My grade school years in Moses Lake held some happy memories. They were filled with arrowhead hunting, camping, boating, a trip to Disneyland, Las Vegas, Mexico, backyard picnics, a trip to Canada via the San Juan Islands, playing for hours and hours with neighborhood kids, helping Father work on boats, hunting for polliwogs in the little pond at the end of the street, selling subscriptions to newspapers, gathering thunder eggs on Red Top Mountain, a trip with my big brother to the World's Fair in Seattle. On the outside, we appeared to be a normal family. On the inside, it was a prison run by a very strict warden.

I learned at an early age to get what I wanted by any means available, including cheating. If there were something that I wanted in my life, I would find a way to "win" it. One summer, when I was eight years old, I had a job going door-to-door asking people to subscribe to the newspaper. In order to motivate the sales force, the paper had a contest for who could get the most subscriptions. I wanted to win this contest and make my father proud of me. After being repeatedly turned down at the door, I decided that to win at this game, I needed a better way to get subscriptions. I wasn't a lousy salesman; I was going to win.

I noticed that many people had their name and address on their mailbox, and it wasn't long before I was filling in the subscription sheets with names right off the boxes. This worked extremely well. The first year I did it, I won third place in the subscription contest. I had actually planned on winning first place, but I ended up coming in third.

My father did not attend my third place winning ceremony. He was busy making Eddie level the backyard because of poor grades. Eddie had all Father's attention.

It was about this time that Eddie decided he was not going to eat peas. One night, he asked permission to eat in our bedroom. Father had left the dinner table early to get back to work building a wooden boat in the garage. Mom said yes, he could eat in the bedroom, and soon this became a regular routine. Father always forced us to clean our plates, but since he had started building boats in the garage, he would eat rapidly and then go to the garage to work. Mom, on the other hand, was easier to convince.

Once in the bedroom, Eddie would take the food that he did not want to eat and put it in an old camera of Mom's, a brownie box camera. This went on for a long time. When the camera would get full, he would empty it out in the backyard. When I figured out what he was doing, he allowed me to do the same thing, although there was not much that I did not eat.

He was finally busted by the old man. Father caught him with the camera out in the yard. When first confronted, he lied. Things get kind of blurry around watching Eddie get whipped, but I clearly remember the look on Father's face. Just before exploding, his tongue went over his lower teeth and pushed his bottom lip out. That was the sign. After the lip, he took off his belt and began whipping Eddie and saying things like, "You little bastard, you will not lie to me ever again! Look what you did to your mother's camera." He had ahold of Eddie's left arm with his left hand while he whipped him. We were never allowed to eat in the bedroom again. Eddie took all the blame and never indicated that I had any involvement.

My biggest blessing was my brother Eddie. Father was so busy teaching him that he seldom had time to notice what I was up to. In my view, Father was beyond disciplining Eddie; he was mean and vicious to him.

To ensure that Eddie would get the backyard leveled, Father drove a steel stake in the ground. He hooked one end of a chain to the stake and the other to Eddie's leg. That did not last long because the neighbors complained. The police came and told Father he couldn't do that. He replied, "He's my son, and I'll do what I want with him." The police backed off, and Father removed the chain. It still had an impact on us all.

Father's ways of teaching were unique in that he believed that if children understood the right way to do something, they would automatically do it. The consequences he imposed were so severe that they ensured obedience. He used the same theory in training the dog, Mom, or any of us. Eddie always seemed to be first in line and first noticed or caught.

When I was eight, we were given a beagle named Suzie. She had puppies, and we kept one. His name was Rebel. Father took Suzie and the other puppies out for a ride, and the story was he shot them in the desert. He said Suzie was worthless and so were the puppies. Except Rebel. Father picked him out as the one worth saving.

Father started training Rebel at an early age. He beat that dog and dragged him around the yard on a rope. He was always mad at that dog. Rebel eventually learned what to do and not do, but it was clear his spirit was gone. He always watched Father. He was lucky one day and got hit by a car and died. The funny thing about that dog was that he acted totally loyal to Father.

For his part, Father never seemed attached to anything. So, when he said he would kill us if we did not behave, I believed him.

I always believed that some day he would take me out in the desert, kill me, and bury me.

Watching Rebel go through his training with Father was shocking, frightening, and burned into my memory. If I were a "bad boy," this could and would happen to me, too. My response was anger, which protected me from feeling the fear. The fear was too much to think about, too much for me to handle at the time.

Father appeared emotionless, unpredictable, and dangerous. It was as though there was always a game with Father. The game for me was "out of sight, out of mind". I spent lots of energy hiding from my dad, escaping attention. I was an observer. I studied Father's moods, moves, and attitudes. I studied everyone, teachers, siblings, neighbors.

At the same time, I worshipped my father as a god. I loved how he could fix anything. I liked his love of cars. I treasured the few times I had him all to myself. And I feared him. I was drawn to him like a moth to a flame. The closer I got to him, the more it hurt. Distance was a good thing.

I was not always fast enough to avoid looking down the barrel of Father's anger. The following summer, when I was nine years old, I discovered my bicycle tire was flat. I could see everyone was too busy to help me. I decided that since I had seen tires pumped up before, I could do it myself. I was big enough. I pushed my bike three blocks to the little store. I stuck the hose on the stem, just as I'd seen grown-ups do. It was more difficult getting the two pieces together than I had imagined, but I did it. Finally, I could hear the air going inside the tire. I was doing it!

I was daydreaming about how great I was when suddenly my world exploded. The noise of the tire popping shocked me out of my reverie. Something was terribly wrong. I pushed my bike home and put it out behind the house. "What happened?" kept ringing through my mind. "Why did this happen to me?"

At about 5:30, I was taking my bath, and I could hear Father's voice asking where I was. Mom said I was bathing. "SO, YOU WANNA TELL ME WHAT HAPPENED?" his voice rang out, as he opened the bathroom door.

I froze. I was petrified to the bone. The one rule I knew was that playing stupid was always a great defense. I'm sure I had the deer in the headlight look on my face, as I stammered, "I don't know..."

He grabbed my arm, pulled me from the tub, and dragged me, wet and naked, into the dining room. He was talking the whole time about me hiding the things I did wrong, that the tire was no big deal, that it was the hiding it I needed to be punished for. Mom was sitting in the living room, and Eddie and Jenny were in their bedrooms as I was paraded along, naked and exposed.

His voice was cold and piercing. "This is for lying," he said as he took his belt and whacked my butt. I remember arguing and trying to protect myself with my hand.

Each time I think of one of the whippings I received, there are overwhelming memories of all the different whippings I got while in Moses Lake. It was not often, I was always watchful and got caught maybe four times a year, but I remember them all.

It was not uncommon to be riding in the car and have Father reach over the front seat and punch someone for doing something that irritated him, things like talking, touching the back of his seat, making any noise. Reading Father's moods was impossible. One moment we could be kids playing, and he was fine. Then, without notice, he would be irritated by the slightest noise or mistake.

There were too many things to be careful of: eating with your mouth open, eating too fast, talking too much, touching the back of the seat he was sitting in, him not being able to find his tools, Mom cooking a bad meal, a dirty dish in the cupboard, a hair in the food, and on and on and on.

Father was a gun loaded with anger, and I always watched to see where it was pointing. Every day someone was in trouble, mostly Eddie, then Mom, then me, seldom Al, and even less Jenny.

I had a best friend, Steven Earl. I couldn't risk inviting him to my house, but I loved going to his home. They had animals: a cow, some chickens, and goats. It was different being at Steven's. There was no threat of violence. It was not something that was talked about, but just being there I knew nobody was going to get hurt.

Our friendship did not last long. After five or six months, in the middle of 5th grade, Father announced we were moving to Las Vegas. This time Mom didn't argue. She didn't want to make Father angry.

The air base was closing, and the economy had collapsed in Moses Lake. Father's boat building and repair business was on its last legs.

Father read books every day and learned about everything through reading. He had read up on Las Vegas and was sure this was the answer to his dreams. He had taught himself to count cards to beat the casinos at "Black Jack."

Father purchased an early fifties International truck with a lime green cab and a big orange box on the back. It was our personal moving van. He also ordered a brand new 1965 Volvo station wagon. We picked it up in Seattle when it arrived from Sweden. It was only a short time before we moved to Las Vegas.

It was a short stay. Father soon discovered that the good jobs were controlled by unions, and it made him angry to have to go through the unions for work. We were only there a couple of weeks when he sent Mom to Tonopah, a couple hundred miles northwest of Las Vegas, to find work. She got a job waiting tables right away. Before the second month's rent was due, the rest of us packed up the old truck and joined her in Tonopah.

Surviving in Tonopah

Tonopah was a small mining town high in the Nevada desert. We moved into a trailer park, with all six of us living in an 8' by 40' mobile home. There were two bedrooms and a bright blue fold-down couch in the living room. Eddie and I slept on the couch. We ate our meals in our laps. We spent our time outside, except to eat and sleep.

When we arrived in Tonopah, I decided I would be called "Don" from that day forward. "Lee" was weak and sensitive; "Don" was tough and strong.

Mom worked at the Tonopah Club, the largest casino in town. Father got a job writing keno tickets. It only lasted a few days. To hear Father tell it, nobody was doing anything right, and he had to quit. He could not work with people who were so stupid.

In a couple of months, we were able to move into an old adobe house on the edge of town. Father soon moved Grandma up from Moses Lake, as well, and set up her trailer on the north side of the house. It was not more than ten feet from our house to Grandma's trailer. Father went right to work hooking it up to water, sewer, and electricity. He put insulated skirting around the bottom. Nothing was too good for Grandma.

Tonopah had a weekly newspaper. I had had lots of experience with newspapers and had helped Eddie deliver papers for years. On Friday afternoons, as soon as school was out, everyone raced to the newspaper office to buy a handful of papers for ten cents each and then resell them for twenty-five cents. I was alive selling papers in the bars, restaurants, casinos, and to anyone on the street. It was a dream come true. In about an hour I would earn between $3.00 and $5.00. I loved talking to people who liked me.

Father struggled to find a source of income in the old mining town. Eddie had always delivered newspapers, and Father decided that he would work with Eddie building a big newspaper route. It started out with just the Review Journal from Las Vegas. It was an evening paper that we delivered in the mornings. In only a few months until Father had secured the delivery route for the Las Vegas Sun, too. It was a morning newspaper, and we delivered them both. Eddie and I would rubber band all the papers and ride with Father, helping deliver them.

Delivering newspapers was a reliable source of income. Eddie had purchased a used Honda 50 for driving to school. It was the coolest thing I had ever seen, a beautiful machine with loads of chrome and bright red paint. It was decided that Eddie would deliver some of the newspapers with his new purchase. I would ride with Father while doing the larger portion of the route. I thought that Father and I were going to bond, doing this work together, but instead, on the first morning, a man backed out of his driveway and cut a hole in the side of Father's Volvo. The repairs were slow, and Father was so focused on how screwed he was because of the accident, I lost my interest in bonding.

Bad luck followed Father, and it followed me, too. Our house was arranged so that you could run a complete circle inside the house. It was great fun chasing each other through the house. On one occasion, I was running from Al and Jenny, having the chase of a lifetime. We were laughing, giggling and shouting.

As I left our bedroom, I slammed the door behind me. The next thirty seconds were an eternity. I was at the top of my game when the door made a banging sound as it closed. In the same instant, I heard Father's 4' x 8' mirror, temporarily propped against the wall, bang into the wall and hit the floor. It broke into three pieces.

There was nowhere to hide. Al and Jenny both pointed out how much trouble I was in. "Father is going to kill you," they said. It was at that moment that I made the decision never to play without being careful. I did get my butt beaten, but more than that, I decided it was not safe to play.

From the time we moved to Tonopah, there was a difference in Father. Previously, he had been mean and explosive. He had hit Mom sometimes, but mostly he was threatening. His use of the belt was excessive, but not brutal. He threatened to leave, but seldom did.

I don't know that I can put the changes into words. For me, I went from fearing being in trouble to fearing for my life. When Father would explode, it got beyond my imagination. On one hand, we delivered newspapers, hunted for ghost towns, looked for purple bottles in the desert, played in the sand dunes, hunted deer, and chased wild horses. On the other hand, there were the cruel, weird, and unbelievable punishments.

One day, just after I had started sixth grade, Father let out a yell from his bedroom, "All of you get your asses in here right now! You're all gonna see what can happen when you don't do what you're told."

Just the tone of his voice was enough to overwhelm me. I was standing in my bedroom at the time. All four of us were in there.

Eddie led the way, and I was the last to walk through the closet connecting our room to our parents' bedroom.

It was like walking into a fog, all senses numbed to the point of elimination. The smell of cigarette smoke lingered in the air. It was a cloudy day, and the only window in the bedroom was covered.

The bedroom door was open with light shining in from the kitchen. The silhouette of Mom being hung from the top of the door like a side of beef hanging in a meat locker was my first image of what was about to happen. Father stood near the head of his bed. In his hands was a leather belt, doubled over.

All of us walked into Mom and Father's bedroom, with me staying as far away as possible. I could see the silver of the handcuffs holding Mom's hands together. Then I could see the nail holding the cuffs on the top of the door. It was like being in a fog. It was not really real, just like a movie that I kept hoping would be over soon.

Father's words were difficult to hear. They seemed distant and blurred. "Now I want all of you to pay attention. This is what will happen to you if you ever cross me."

With that, he picked up the belt and struck her butt. He repeated that this was the only way people learned, by first "getting their attention."

Mom screamed each time the belt connected with her butt and thighs. She begged him to stop, whining, "I will be good," over and over. Her sobs were louder and more painful with each whack of the belt. Father told her to shut up and take her medicine.

I could not escape the terror. But I could control feeling anything. Father had taught me well. He always gave us our haircuts and demanded that we hold perfectly still. This was a case where his training served me. I could control every part of my body, completely, allowing nothing in or out.

To stop Mom's screaming, Father picked up an old towel and used it as a gag, tying it behind her head. I could see blood penetrating her pants. Standing there frozen stiff, I waited for it all to stop. I could not measure the time, but after the gag, it was clear Father had made his point, and he stopped hitting her. He turned and looked at all of us and said, "Now you know what will happen if you cross me."

No one made a sound. We turned and walked back through the closet into our bedroom. No one spoke. Eddie lay on his bed, and Al and Jenny disappeared outside. I crawled up to my bed, the third tier of a triple bunk bed. I had put up a curtain around my bed and installed a shelf against the wall. There would be no dinner or watching television. The house would be silent the remainder of the evening and into the night. I would lay there and rock myself back and forth waiting to fall asleep.

I could understand that Father finding a hair in his food or the food not being cooked properly would justify him throwing the entire meal against the wall. I could understand him breaking all the dining room chairs because we behaved like animals and did not deserve to sit on nice furniture. I could understand that children need to be taught and that all he was doing was getting our attention. But, I never have understood what Mom did to deserve being handcuffed. Up until now I could figure out the sense of the things Father did. But after we moved to Tonopah, the violence escalated and logic was out the door.

Al and I joined the Boy Scouts of America. There were weekly meetings and all the cool kids in school belonged. I loved

Boy Scouts. It was a warm and friendly place to be. Sharing a bedroom with two brothers and a sister left little space for me. The Boy Scouts offered a level playing field. At Christmas time we would gather trees to sell, and in the summer we would go camping.

It was in the summer between 6th and 7th grade that we went to Stove Pipe Wells in Death Valley for a Scout Jamboree. I had never had so much fun, swimming, camping, hiking, playing, and shopping. It was in the gift shop that I found the most beautiful bull whip I had ever seen. It was six feet long and had a carved wooden handle. I loved how it felt in my hand, so powerful, commanding, and unafraid.

It was late Sunday afternoon when we returned from the scouting weekend. Mom greeted Al and me at the bus and took us home. I could hardly wait to show off my prized possession. Father was sitting in the living room in his chair. When I passed through the living room, Father asked what I had in my hand. I froze. The tone of his voice sent chills tingling down my spine.

With hesitation I answered, "A bull whip." There was a long silence before Father spoke. "That is not a toy," he said. His words hung in the air. "Bring it here."

"I will keep this," he said. "Matter of fact, this is perfect for issuing punishment."

I was frozen in time. Father yelled, "Everyone into the living room!" As Al, Jenny, Eddie, and Mom entered the room, their eyes were on the bull whip in Father's hand. "You can all thank your brother for providing me with this handsome new whip," he said. The looks, the mumbling, and the feeling of hatred were clear in my mind.

That whip was around for several years, more than I care to remember. Father frayed the leather end and could easily peel skin from any part of a fully clothed body. It was bad enough watching Father punish anyone, but using the bull whip added a pain that I carried deep in my soul. I withdrew from any relationship with anyone else in the family.

While we were in Tonopah, my father started countless projects and never finished a single one. He was so smart that he could never really do anything. All the half-done or unfinished projects in his life were evidence that before he completed anything, he would see the end and find it pointless to finish. He never experienced finishing anything.

He put in a rental trailer on the other side of Grandma's trailer. It created income, but tenants seemed a bit of a challenge. He invented a telephone answering machine, but then found they were already on the market. He built a picnic table in the backyard that was always half finished. It was literally half a table. The wooden top was round, but he never completed the second half of the top.

He started his own taxi business that was successful to the degree a taxi business could be in a town of 1,000 people. He developed his own mine claim, which would give him the land under our house virtually for free. He made an agreement to purchase the house we lived in. After a year of making his $50 per month payments, he stopped because the owner of the house had not filed the paperwork for the mining claim. He declared that until the paperwork on the land was straightened out, he would make no more payments. It turned out that he could have filed the paperwork as easily as the landowner, but instead he chose to be angry. We lived in the house for six years and never owned it.

He started building an elaborate addition to the house, completing the foundation and outside structure on a house he did not own. We hand cut and oiled each shake for the roofing, an incredible project, but we only completed about a third of the roof before running out of shakes.

He started to rebuild a Model A pickup. He built his own camper with a rounded top, but again, never finished it. It was usable, but not finished. Father started many projects, but for one reason or another, they all ended unfinished.

During the years between elementary school and my junior year in high school, there were numerous events of violence in our house. Eddie was the center of attention for the worst of the physical beatings, but as I entered my teen years, there was more focus on me. When I was 13, Father taught me to adjust his back. He would lay on the coffee table, and I would pretend I was the chiropractor. I would crack his back, adjusting the vertebrae. He had walked with a limp since his hospital stay at sixteen, and complained of tremendous pain in his back. He went to chiropractors when possible, but that was always at least a hundred mile drive.

With all the training I was getting, I decided I would be a chiropractor myself. School had always been difficult for me. I talked so much that I seldom heard what anyone else was saying, and my grades reflected my lack of paying attention. I had learned to cheat and charm my way through school. My focus was on the tests, not the learning. It was amazing how I could pass a test and not know any of the material.

The thought of being a chiropractor lit me up. My grades improved in school, and there seemed to be a way out for me. Then one Sunday in the middle of summer, Father had me adjust his back. I started with the lumbar roll on the floor, then he moved to the coffee table where I began adjusting his upper back. I was quite confident in my skills and ability. Father was busy giving instructions, higher, lower, harder, more twist. All of a sudden, he exploded with anger, "You son of a bitch, you just hurt me!"

His words rang in my ears as he stood up. He ordered me to lay on the table, telling me how I needed to know what it was like for a patient when they are hurt by me not being careful. Everything was surreal. As I lay on the table with him tweaking my back, the physical pain was nothing in comparison to seeing my future disappear.

The following summer, Eddie graduated from high school, joined the Navy, and left home. His leaving created a completely new relationship for me with my father. I was no longer able to hide behind Eddie and all his problems.

At fourteen, I got caught stealing a bottle of wine, and the police told me I had to tell Father. At home, I sat waiting for him to return from a taxi call. I sat on the couch frozen to total numbness. When Father returned, I waited for him to sit down, and then I blurted out, "I was caught stealing a bottle of wine today."

His initial response was, "What else have you been stealing?"

I hesitated and looked in my bag of secrets. There were lots of things I could offer up to appease him, but words came slowly. "Once a bag of peanuts?" I said.

In that moment, it was over. He began by reaching over and striking the tops of my legs with his closed fist. All the time he was yelling, "You worthless bastard, you no good son of a bitch."

It went on and on. From the legs, he moved to the face, and then started whacking me with a wooden cane. He was so mad, I thought he was going to kill me. I ended up lying on the floor bleeding from a gash on the back of my head. "I am not raising a thief, I will kill you first," he said.

Summer came again, and this time I had three jobs, plus delivering newspapers. I started the mornings at 4:00 am and got my paper route completed by 5:30. Then I went to the Tonopah Club where I bussed tables during the morning rush. I worked 'til 9:00 am, when I would head for the construction site at the hospital where I did cleanup work until 4:00 pm. Then I went across the street where I washed dishes until 9:00 pm. It was perfect! I had money, was never home, and really enjoyed what I was doing.

Before the summer was over, I decided that the pressure of being caught by Father was more than I needed to deal with. A friend of mine was going to live with his father and invited me to come along. The construction was complete at the hospital, and the crew had returned to Reno. I decided this was my opportunity to get out from under Father. First I traveled to Reno, where I hoped the construction company would help me. They were not interested in a 15-year-old runaway. Next, I traveled to Elko where I found my friend James living with his father.

Living in Elko only lasted a few months. I started out living with James, his dad, and his dad's girlfriend. They were Native American. We hunted rabbits, had a car, and attended high school.

Tattooing was a cool thing, and a boy name Eddie Ellison said he knew how to get tattoos. We had been drinking beer for hours, and that sounded like a great idea to me. I wrote the letters L-O-V-E on my forearm and put the initials JB below. All my life I had written the word "love" on everything. I had doodled the word since I started writing. JB was Julie Bretts, the girl I wanted to be in love with. She did not even know I existed.

Eddie did not complete the tattoo. He first did an outline of each letter and then started filling in the centers. He completed the V and E. The L and O were only outlines. The JB looked like two small straight marks below "LOVE." I regretted that day every day for thirty years. It was proof of how stupid I was.

Five years ago the tattoo was professionally removed. Before the birth of my daughter, I was told by a friend who had been severely abused herself that the tattoo had the story of my life in it. The L and O were empty, and the V and E were full. The first half of my life there was no love inside me, but the good news was the second half was going to be full. That fit for me and gave me hope that I would not live my life without knowing love.

Drinking was a big part of James' lifestyle and did not work for me. I soon moved in with a family in town, but that only lasted a week. Then I met Leroy and Philip. They were from New Mexico. They had a small house by the railroad tracks, and we survived by stealing anything we could get our hands on. Life with them was exciting at first, but soon I could see that I was going nowhere.

It had been four months since I left home. I called Mom and asked if I could come home. I was tired of the partying. I tired quickly of being with people who drank, and I was scared to death of drugs. Mom sent me a bus ticket home. It took most of a day to return. All the way, I fantasized how wonderful it would be to be home.

In only a couple of weeks I realized the depth of my mistake. Nothing had changed at home. Al and Jenny still hated me. Father watched everything I was doing, and Mom was oblivious to it all.

I called Philip in Elko and made my plans to run away again. I borrowed enough money from Grandma for a bus ticket and planned my escape. I arrived in Elko via Greyhound, and things were not going well there. Philip had been arrested, and I heard the police were looking for me. I hid out in the attic of the little house by the tracks, but it did not take the police long to find me. When I came down, I found my parents waiting outside for me. It was a long ride back to Tonopah. Father was very clear that I would not run away again.

I got back to doing my paper route. Father allowed me no life outside the family. I was not to leave early for school, for lunch I was to come home, and after school I was to come immediately home. I would be allowed one hour for homework, and the balance of my time was to be spent working on the addition to the house or any other project that Father chose.

I tried hard to please Father. It seemed that the harder I tried, the worse things would get. I would get bored, and my mind would wander. Whether it was holding a board while he cut it, or hand cutting shakes for the roof, everything about working bored me eventually, and I would daydream about better times. During the next year, I resigned myself to the fact that I was a prisoner with no hope of parole. There were beatings and violence. There were family outings and Eddie's marriage. I survived everything remembering the dog Rebel and how lucky he was to have been hit by a car. I too hoped to get that lucky some day.

During the summer between my sophomore and junior years of high school, I got to work construction with Eddie. He was home from the Navy, having been caught stealing. It turned out that Father had been his advisor in the thefts, and he had shipped lots of the loot home before being caught.

Eddie and I traveled to several different towns over the summer. It was great being away from Father, sometimes for days on end. I saved up my money and purchased Father's 1966 Dodge Coronet. It had been the taxi, and now the business was closed. Father had his pickup truck. I cherished that old car, yet I still owed Father money on my purchase. I was allowed to take the car to school on special occasions.

In late August, Father became very sick and almost died from a perforated ulcer. He was treated locally and then flown to Reno where he spent two months recovering. I was left home with Grandma. It was perfect! I went to school and enjoyed working on Father's house addition project.

I did not see Father for the months he was in the hospital. In October, the family returned home. I helped Father load up the pickup and a trailer with all his prized possessions. He was headed to San Diego to sell what he could to raise some funds. The stay in the hospital had taken all the money Mom and Dad had, and they owed more now than ever before.

Father returned in a couple of weeks. I was working on the new addition when he walked in. I had built the framing, installed it, and then applied the sheetrock over the frame. I was beyond proud of myself. I knew I had accomplished something important to Father.

To my disbelief, Father picked up a round, black electrical cord and proceeded to give me the worst whipping I could ever imagine. All the time he was whipping, Father said that what I had done created more work for him than if I had done nothing at all. He wanted me to remember that it is better to do nothing than to do something poorly.

It was just before Thanksgiving when Father, Mom, Al, and Jenny loaded up the car and headed back to San Diego. They would be home as soon as they could, and Father was very clear in his instructions regarding his pickup. I was not to use it other than for necessary trips. He had the snow chains on it and wanted them removed if they started to come apart.

It was Christmas Eve when they arrived home. There were several inches of snow on the ground. The air was crisp and clean. I heard the car pull up and rushed out to greet everyone. Father immediately directed me to help Al and Jenny unload the car. The trunk was packed. While unloading, I asked Al, "What did they get for me?"

His response was quick and sharp, "What makes you think they would get you anything?"

On my last trip into the house, Father asked why I had removed the chains from the truck. My response was quick and clean, "They were falling apart, so I removed them." The look on his face was the first warning.

"Go get them and bring them in here," his words commanded. I knew I was in trouble. I had always kept secrets, things I did that Father never knew about. When the possibility of being in trouble was present, it was like opening Pandora's box, massive amounts of secrets, and if any one of them were to be exposed, I would be annihilated.

As I walked into the kitchen with the chains in my hand, I could tell Father had the look of annihilation in his eyes. I tried to argue, but to no avail. I was guilty, and he had had enough of my deception.

It started with punching and proceeded to get really violent, with him slamming my arm against door jams trying to break it. It ended with me lying by the front door next to the gun cabinet. Now, one thing I knew was Father's rule about guns: unloaded guns were worthless.

I watched as his hand reached into the cabinet and grabbed the grip of his nickel-plated Smith and Wesson 38. The words still ring in my mind, "The only way to deal with you is to kill you." Before the words were completely out of his mouth, I had my hand on the door handle and the door open. He would not get off a shot. I ran and ran. I asked neighbors for help, but they were frightened of Father and refused to help me.

An older friend was a dishwasher in the Tonopah Club. I went to him, and he gave me his coat and told me to get out of town. I went to a gas station where a schoolmate was working and asked him to hide me. I lay under the counter with a loaded sawed-off 22 rifle against my chest. I lay there for several hours, until Roy had to close the station. I gave Roy back the gun and took the short walk to my friend Bobby's house. Nobody was home, so I settled into an empty car in the driveway. It was cold, but soon I fell asleep. I was jarred awake by the opening of the car door.

"What are you doing?" It was Bobby and his sister. I said I just wanted to get warm and I would be on my way. They invited me into the house. Their parents were gone.

Mr. and Mrs. Barns arrived home to find me sitting in the kitchen. They told me I would stay in the guestroom and in the morning they would talk to the judge. They assured me that my father would never touch me again. The next morning, Christmas Day, they called the judge, and he came in the afternoon to see me. With one look at me, he said he would protect me. I had a broken ear drum, broken teeth, and bruises over my entire body.

Two days later, Mrs. Barns took me to the courthouse. I went into the judge's chambers where my parents were seated. I sat between them, and my father asked only one question, "Is this what you really want?"

I was quick to answer, "Yes." That was all that was said to me. My father argued that he should not have to pay support for me, but to no avail.

Three days later, I was on my way to the Nevada State Children's Home in Carson. A social worker drove me the two hundred miles. The Children's Home consisted of seven homes, each housing 10 children. There was a gym, bowling alley, tennis courts, a recreation room, and a commissary. There were 30 girls and 40 boys. Each house had live-in "parents" and a relief parent for two days a week.

I did not like the Children's Home from the get-go. Even though it was safe, and nobody was going to beat me, I was better than all this. I just wanted to get out on my own. I liked getting everything they had to offer, but I felt I was special in my needs.

There were lots of perks at the Children's Home: Christmas gifts, good food to eat, a clothing allowance. But I saw myself as better than anyone there. Most had been there a long time; none were there for being beaten. I considered myself different, mostly better. I believed I deserved special privileges, like driving and owning a car, coming home when I wanted, working when I wanted, and doing what I wanted. After all, I was there because I had been beaten....

On one hand, I was happy to have a place to live, on the other I was very angry that they could not see how hurt I was. I wanted someone to see I was special. I needed to be loved, and I was busy proving nobody could love me. The parents in the Home were paid to care for me, but I saw that if I wanted their love, I would have to be the way they wanted me to be. If not, they were just guards in an open prison.

The tattoo on my arm said everything... "LOVE." I wanted to be loved. I wanted acknowledgement for being hurt, almost killed. I wanted to be protected from it ever happening again. I wanted to be known.

When I first arrived at the Children's Home, I was extremely well-behaved. For me it was mostly a mechanical relationship. I knew they did not love me, it was just their job to take care of me. So I was never available to the love they might have offered. I was defensive, always watching for how I could get my share of whatever was available. I kept myself isolated emotionally from any connection with anyone there. I hung out with kids from town; I got jobs on my own. I did all right in school so I would not be hassled about grades.

I lived at the Children's Home for just about one year. Right after arriving at the Home, I got a job, first in a restaurant, then working construction. I made new friends. I purchased a car with the help of my boss. Life was very good in my eyes. I met and dated nice girls, but relationships were short-lived for me. I was finally free, and nothing was going to get in my way.

Making it on my Own

On December 9, 1971, I turned 18. I had been at the Children's Home nearly a year, and now I had the choice to move out or to stay at the Home until I finished high school. I still did not like the Children's Home.

I did not care about anybody at the Home, and I knew they did not care about me. I believed they were there just because they had a job to do, or they were stupid.

The Children's Home had rules. I was expected to save half of my paychecks, be home at 10:00 pm, and do chores like cleaning house and helping on Saturdays. They did not want me to drive my car, because of liability, even though I already had a driver's license.

I told myself that I could make my own decisions and manage myself better on my own.

Having grown up in an abusive home and then being free was a lot to be responsible for. Part of me wanted to stay and enjoy the advantages of the Children's Home. Another part of me wanted to get out on my own and take care of myself because no one else would.

I waited until after Christmas to go. I intended to get whatever I could from the Home. I imagined the presents at Christmas would make me feel good.

I didn't think about the previous Christmas. If it crossed my mind, I blanked it out. If the only feeling one can have is anger, rage, or hatred toward something, I was better off being numb, feeling nothing.

I taught myself how I was supposed to feel in response to Christmas. I pretended to be happy, friendly, and generous. I generated feelings that I thought I was supposed to feel. Nothing was ever real, and as long as nothing happened to surprise or scare me, I was fine. If something did happen, and the volcano that simmered under the surface were to show itself, I would quickly rein it back in.

One of the tricks I learned was the ability to forget any unpleasant memories and feelings. It was as if I carried a large suitcase in which I stored unwanted feelings. To open it was sheer terror, more than I could handle. I would stuff any feeling I did not want into the suitcase and forget it. Then I would smile and think I was enjoying life to the fullest. Any time I felt worthless, angry, or frightened, I would open the suitcase and stuff more bad feelings in there.

By the time I lived at the Children's Home, I was a pro at this technique of always feeling good, no matter what. I did not cry. I would act crazy, if it would get me something, but I was always in control, always, always. In the secret of my mind, I was always controlling everything that was happening. I had complete power over myself and my feelings. I carried that invisible suitcase with me at all times.

As I walked away from the restrictions and safety of the Children's Home, I couldn't allow myself to feel the loneliness, fear, and confusion I was carrying inside. I had no one to trust but myself, no rules to live by but my own. And underneath it all was the deep-seated fear of being found out, the terror that my father had had good cause to beat me, and it was only a matter of time before I would be found out.

I was screaming inside, but I never allowed myself to hear it. It was silent, very high pitched, and would only have been heard by the animals that would understand my pain and fear. If anyone had heard them, the words I was screaming would have been, "PLEASE HELP ME..."

In mid-January, I packed my suitcase, put on a shit-eating grin, and walked out of the Children's Home and into the world.

My boss at the construction company was a kind man, and he gave me a place to stay until I could find something more permanent for myself. He was divorced and lived in a small tract house with two teenagers still at home. I slept on the living room couch. It was very short term, but it was safe.

He owned the company with his brother and made a modest living. I was a laborer and did anything I was told, from setting concrete forms to cleaning up. I loved working hard and was allowed to keep my own hours. My boss gave me a great deal of freedom. He encouraged me to attend high school and graduate. While I was still at the Children's Home, he had loaned me $150 to buy a car from my friend Paul. It was a '63 Ford Galaxy two-door hardtop with a white exterior and blue interior. It had mag wheels and was raised in the rear. To me, it was the coolest car anywhere. I felt like a million bucks driving it.

With that car, a solid job, and a roof over my head, I had made it. I was living on my own. I was going places. I was destined for something big.

Immediately, my thoughts turned to Father. My success would not be complete without Father seeing how I had made it. He was God, and if I could get his "You did good, son," everything would be okay. I just wanted to hear that I had gotten it right and that he recognized I had value and worth.

I had been at my boss' house barely a week when I decided to call my brother Eddie in San Diego. I found that Father, Mom, Al, and Jenny were now living behind a small store front downstairs from Eddie and his wife. Father had moved there to be close to good medical help, and he and Eddie had gone into business together.

I called and talked to Father. He said he would be happy to see me any time that I was in the area.

I immediately loaded up my car and headed for San Diego. I drove all night and arrived as the sun was coming up. I found the store and went around back. I entered from the alley and went down a few steps into what was used as a kitchen. Father was in the next room, lying on a mattress. He always spent a lot of time lying down because of the way his back bothered him. There was an uneasiness in the room, like everyone was holding their breath, Al, Jenny and Mom. I walked into the room slowly, wondering if I had made a huge mistake.

His first words were, "How you doing?"

"Fine..."

"How was the drive down?"

"Fine...." In the back of my mind, I was rattling on, "Dad, I have a cool car! And a job and a place to live. I am a success! Please see me as a success."

I was quiet and let my father lead the conversation. He explained that they were only in this apartment temporarily. He made a phone call. He had hooked up wires to a telephone booth in front of the store. He sent my mom out to deposit a dime and dial the number. Then Father picked up the line he had installed in his room and took the call. He talked to Jim Walter, the owner of the building, and invited him to breakfast. He could not come. "You know," he said, "I have been thinking about the money you left on the wall." As I was growing up, we used to keep track of our earnings on a piece of paper taped to the wall. "These barrettes are the newest thing on the market," he said. He handed me several strings of leather hair barrettes. They were in the shape of cowboy hats with a round stick through them for attaching to the hair. "If you would like to triple your investment, I will give you your money in barrettes."

"That sounds great to me," I said. I really did not want the barrettes, but I could see it would make him happy. In the end, they turned out to be difficult to sell, but eventually I was able to unload them for a couple hundred dollars.

He brought up the old Dodge I had left in Tonopah. It was mine if I paid off the $225 I owed him for it. I agreed to pay it when I could, and he gave me the keys.

My father talked about Eddie, how he and Sue lived upstairs and some of the stupid things he had done. He'd wrecked his car, gotten drunk and threw up all over the place, lit a firecracker and dropped it in a bag of fireworks, setting off the whole bag. Father liked pointing out how "dumb" Eddie was.

Al and Jenny went off to school.

Father and I were square, and I had only been there for an hour and a half. A feeling of comfort and relief washed over me. I knew that I had done him wrong by going to the judge, and I felt forgiven. I relaxed and felt confident that it was all behind me.

I loved feeling good, so much so that I would avoid looking at the reality, that my father was a loser, always blaming someone else for his failures. I was on the inside circle now. I was not a target of his anger or rage.

Eddie awoke, and he, Father, and I went for breakfast at a nearby restaurant. Father continued to direct the conversation. He was proud of the business he and Eddie were in. They were doing great selling plaster of paris statues from Mexico and black velvet paintings and hair barrettes.

He looked at Eddie. "I think we should go to Mexico and get another load of plaster," he said, meaning statues and piggy banks.

"I agree, Dad," Eddie replied.

"This time, if we go further north, I am sure we can make ten times our money," he went on.

"You're right, Dad," said Eddie.

I was feeling good. I felt that I had rejoined the family, so to speak, now that I was out on my own and successful.

I was confident about joining the conversation. I began to express my opinions on their business plans and the right way to market the barrettes. I offered my insights about making money. About halfway through breakfast, Father exploded. "You self-righteous little cocksucker!" My body froze, and I started planning my escape.

I did not respond. I just swallowed and looked away. From that moment on, I was numb. We returned to the house, and I said my good-byes. I got in my car and began the 600-mile drive back to Carson. It was a long trip. I was tired from not sleeping the night before.

I went back to school and back to work. I loved working with the construction crew. I started early in the morning and was in class by 10:30 am. My boss was supportive, but if he was taking me under his wing, I didn't notice. I was headed someplace on my own, and I wasn't stopping for directions.

I looked around and noticed there weren't many older men working in construction. The ones who were seemed to be having problems with drinking and with their lives. I was doing what I had to, with construction work, to get by for now. Soon I would be on to something better.

This was when I met Al Frost. He was twenty-one and had his own apartment. We agreed to get a trailer together and share the rent. I sold my car and got a '63 Chevy pickup. Our place rapidly became party central, and it was not long before I had lost my job. Graduation was getting close. One thing I was sure of, I was determined to graduate from high school.

Al and I traveled to Tonopah, got the Dodge, and brought it back to Carson. I sold the truck, then immediately wrecked the car, hot-rodding. I was afoot for my high school graduation.

As soon as I had that diploma in my hand, my first thought again was to find Father. It turned out that he and Mom were now working with a carnival in northern California, only a couple hundred miles away. With my diploma in one hand and a pillowcase of clothes in the other, I headed out to the Interstate. I was quick to get rides, and it was late afternoon when I arrived in Redding. I got a ride right to the carnival grounds. I walked right to the booth Father was setting up. His greeting was indifferent. I showed him my diploma, and he responded with, "So, do you want to work?"

I couldn't believe he wanted me to work for him! I worked the entire weekend and caught a ride Monday morning back to Carson. With the money I had earned, I would repair my car and meet them at the next county fair.

It only took two days for me to get my car repaired and be back on the road. I arrived late in the afternoon at the fairgrounds in Turlock, California. It was the first day of the fair, and the booth was already set up. Father showed me how to hustle customers for extra money. It was a ring toss booth. He taught me the pitches. "Throw 'til you win, only 25 cents! Everyone is a winner here!" Father explained to me that when you see someone playing for the big prizes, you make them an offer. You offer to move the big prize to a lower post for five dollars.

The first customer I tried that with won the prize, and I was devastated. Father was pissed.

Father was not feeling well and spent most of his time lying down. The next morning, I helped Mom set up the booth. During the day, we would see Father watching us from different vantage points. After working twelve hours, I had earned all of nine dollars and 25 cents. The pressure was too much, so I told Mom good-bye, got in my car, and returned to Carson. Rejoining my family wasn't going to work.

When I had gone to Tonopah to retrieve the Dodge, Grandma had still been living there in her trailer next to the house. I now decided that helping Grandma would be a great thing. I returned to Tonopah, sold Grandma's trailer and convinced her that living with me was the best thing for both of us.

Grandma was the most loving person I had ever met. She had given me piano lessons for years and years. She was always kind and loving to everyone. Mom and Father had been gone from Tonopah for most of a year and a half, and I was convinced they had abandoned her. I packed her things, and off to Carson we went.

First, I rented a small house, and I worked in a gas station. It was great having Grandma waiting at home every evening.

It was only a month before I discovered I had taken on way too much responsibility. I was a total failure at taking care of

Grandma. I was only concerned with partying. I soon lost my job, and I had trouble paying the rent. I found a less expensive trailer in town and moved Grandma there. I told her I would have to go find work.

A friend, Dennis, and I decided that life on the road would be best. We packed up my car and hit the road. Our first stop was Elko. There we found my old friend Philip and had a place to stay. I began stealing money and gambling with it to try to raise some cash. Philip was married now and working full time, so we were not entertained, and I felt that I would get in trouble if we hung around there for very long. Within a week, we moved on.

My Uncle Harold was in Washington state, so we headed in that direction. It was a week's journey from Elko to Washington, with lots of partying and fun. We arrived in Moses Lake in the late evening. I checked the phone book and did not find my uncle listed. I had a sense that he was living in Ephrata, a smaller town some fifteen miles away. We arrived in Ephrata after the bars had closed, and I drove around looking for anything familiar. Nothing struck a bell. We parked along the street near a park.

In the morning, I awoke to the sound of kids talking outside the car. It was my cousins! I could not believe it, but we had parked right in front of their house. We were welcomed in and given sleeping quarters in the basement.

It was only a couple weeks before Dennis headed home. I got a job working in a gas station and liked living with Uncle Harold and his wife Marsha. I worked the graveyard shift and seldom saw them. There was plenty of food and a warm place to sleep.

I did not give a thought to Grandma or send her money. I felt that she had plenty.

I thought only of myself and how I could get what I thought I deserved. I spent my time working on my car, fixing all the little details. I had it fully repainted. I put cool wheels on it and raised the rear end. I was making it into a cool car.

Moving to Washington had given me a fresh start, but I had not changed. I had started with the best of intentions, but slowly my new world was starting to look like the old one, where I was the problem. The world around me began to get out of control. Bad things began to happen all around me.

Harold and Marsha were now fighting all the time, and things were not going well at work.

I was responsible for the night shift at the Union 76 station. I had been letting my friend Eddy work in the shop, which was not allowed. He should not even have been hanging out at the station, which I let him do all the time. He was a burned-out stoner who I liked and enjoyed hanging out with. One night, things got out of control, and he ran a car into the wall of the station, causing several hundred dollars worth of damage.

Shortly after that incident, a personal friend of my boss stopped in for gas on the way to work. It was early morning, about 6:30 am. He was driving a nice '66 Thunderbird. This was in the days of full service gas stations, and I checked the oil while the car was filling with gas. When I closed the hood, it must not have latched.

He returned about twenty minutes later, just before my boss arrived. He was angry, and the hood of his car was bent up. Apparently, it had flown open as he drove down the road. I was frozen the minute I saw his anger. He yelled at me that I was going to pay.

The boss showed up shortly afterwards and said his insurance would pay for it, but it was the final straw for me. I hated being wrong and would do anything to avoid the feeling of being wrong. At the time I did not realize it, but being in trouble and it clearly being my fault was more than I could deal with.

The only way to escape the feeling was to be punished. That always ended the mental torture that went on in my head. In this case, nobody really punished me. I lived waiting for the other shoe to drop, and it was not dropping. That drove me crazy. I had to get out of there.

I drove to Texas to meet up with Al, Dennis, and another friend, Daryl, who were living with Dennis' aunt in Austin. I was expecting to find fame and fortune. What I found was little work and low wages. Two weeks, and I was ready for somewhere else.

At eighteen, I was immature and simply reacting to life, with no direction or guidance. I saw myself as living under the family curse. When things went wrong, it was someone else's fault. It was never me. I was a victim. There was nothing I could do but start again. It never occurred to me that I had any control over the circumstances of my life or that I could change my life by looking inside myself.

I returned to Carson to find that Grandma was gone. Mom and Father had found her and taken her with them to California. Mom was pregnant, and they had settled down in Tulare. I was lost.

I talked Al into going back to Washington with me. We hit the road and were at Uncle Harold's house in less than twenty-four hours. We arrived to find Harold in the middle of a divorce and moving to another house. We hung around a couple weeks and then went to Al's parents' house. I stayed with them for a few days, but Al's dad clearly did not like me. I returned to Carson and stayed with my friend Art.

Easter weekend we partied all night. I woke up lying in the sand next to a burned out fire and knew I needed to do something different.

On Monday morning, I got Art to take me to the Army recruiter in Reno, and we both signed up for a two-year hitch.

Art and I went through boot camp together and then went our separate ways. I was sent to New Jersey and Art to New Mexico.

I spent the next year in "AIT," Advanced Individual Training. I did well in the school. I was trained to repair electronic communication gear. It took a year to complete my training. During that time, I fell in love with a 32-year-old divorcee, Tammy. She had two children. When the Army gave me orders to go to Germany, I refused, based on the idea that the tour was 18 months and I only had ten months left to serve. Finally, after lots of discussion, I was given orders to Fort Jackson, South Carolina.

During my schooling, I had enjoyed being "slack." My uniforms were tattered and torn. I arrived in South Carolina to find an Army that I had only heard about. Everything was very strict and military. Suddenly I was required to abide by rules I did not remember, and I hated the idea of the strict enforcement of rules. It only took a few days to realize this was not the place for me. I decided that I had had enough and took an unauthorized leave. I knew that at the end of thirty days they would throw me out.

Things never go according to plan. Upon my return, I was told that I would be forgiven, I just had to get my act together. I said I wanted out. "That's simple," replied my First Sergeant, "just disobey a direct order, and you will be out of here in a few days." He ordered me to get in uniform, I refused, and they sent me to the stockade where I served three weeks before being Section Eight discharged, undesirable, with no benefits. I was so glad to be out of the service.

I immediately traveled back to New Jersey and Tammy. I got a room in a rooming house and a job at the Ingersoll-Rand factory. The pay was decent and offered a future that would set me up with my new family. Tammy, however, was different since my return. She always had excuses why I should not come by. It only took me a couple weeks of getting the run-around before I figured out that she was seeing someone else. I caused a scene, got drunk, wrecked my car, and could not go on. I called Eddie and told him my sad story. He told me to sell what was left of my car and fly to San Diego. He would give me a job and a place to stay.

In less than 24 hours, I was in San Diego. Eddie had a motor home rental business and a bottled water route in the beach areas. I was an excellent hand at working on the motor homes and delivering the bottled water. There were three fourplex studio apartments across the street from his house. I rented one of them, and life began to get good again.

Apparently, things were not going well for Eddie in the motor home business. He was in debt, and he and Father came up with an idea for making some quick dough. Soon, they were gone, headed across country on their newest scheme to make money.

I was left with the bottled water route, his rental house, and total freedom. I decided that I deserved to have a nice car. I would do anything for a buck and always felt that I deserved to have nice things. I talked a friend, Sandy, into helping me steal a VW bug. I wanted one that had been baha'd. We went to the university campus, found a car, and kicked in the wing window. I hotwired it and drove it home. I kept it in the garage while I stripped it, then took it to have it painted. It went from bright green to metallic blue. I put different wheels and tires on it. I had purchased an old VW bug and used the registration from it to get license plates for this car. What a great success!

I worked part time for my father's friend, Jim Walter. He peddled Mexican imports. He worked fairs and small communities all over the western United States. One sunny afternoon, I was traveling towards El Cajon, east of San Diego, and was pulled over for speeding.

Once again, I was cursed. A passerby pulled over and told the policeman that the car I was driving was stolen. It had been his neighbor's, and he knew it well because he had fabricated the front bumper himself. Well, from there it is a short story. I was off to jail and out on bail. Lots of questions were asked about all sorts of things that I was connected to, but there was no real proof. I knew when to keep my mouth shut, and this time I did. I hired the cheapest attorney I could find, knowing that I would get no time. It was only my first offense.

It was a few nights later that I met Marian in a neighborhood bar. She had long blond hair, a figure to die for, and a beautiful tan. Most of all, she was friendly and seemed to like me. I got her phone number and asked to call her the next day. We went on a date that night and made love. There was no shame. At 21, it was unlike anything I had ever experienced.

Marian liked something about me. I did not know what, but I knew she saw something of value in me.

I continued traveling and selling for Jim, and Marian joined me on the road.

I clearly remember our first fight. We were traveling in a motor home and had stopped at a campground for the night. Marian had just washed her hair. It was waist length, blond, and beautiful, and washing it was always an event. She had just spent almost an hour and a handful of quarters showering and washing her hair in the campground showers.

It had been a great day for sales. I had $3,000 hidden under the mattress and was feeling really up. We had picked up fried chicken and a quart of milk from the grocery store. We had just finished loading up all the pottery, plaster, and leather we had been selling, and I was going on about what a lucrative day we had. I said, "I cannot believe I have over $3,000 under the mattress!"

Marian said, "It isn't very smart having all that money under the mattress." Instantly, I heard how stupid I was. I exploded. It was as if she had pushed a button that gave me no choice but to defend myself. I threw the paper plate of chicken at her first, then reached over, grabbed the carton of milk, and emptied it on her head.

She yelled at me, "Jesus Christ, what the hell is wrong with you?" I had no explanation. I was surprised by my own actions and started apologizing and trying to justify how much her words had hurt me. She was mad as hell at me, and I waited on her hand and foot until I knew I was out of trouble.

At times like these, when I was feeling really good about what a great guy I was, I was most vulnerable to criticism. At the instant I heard that I was "wrong" or "bad" I went from feeling great to feeling like the worst person on the planet. Being wrong meant I needed to be punished, and I was not aware of anything except that I had to stop her from hurting me. I saw myself as justified in whatever it took to stop her. I did feel bad afterwards, but not like I had done something wrong, just that she had forced me into protecting myself that much. I actually hated Marian for hurting me.

I loved how she made me feel and hated how she made me feel. I was totally at her mercy, and she did not know it.

I had no worth inside me. I found it in work, in my friends, and big time in Marian. I also found the opposite. I was worthless in her parents' eyes and in the eyes of my father. I would constantly bounce in response to my environment.

Violence was about power and control over that environment. Right from the beginning, there was a struggle to control Marian. She gave me worth, and I had to control her so that I wouldn't lose her.

We traveled across northern New Mexico and southern Colorado. It was a dream come true for me. We traveled for almost two months while waiting for my court date. I had pleaded guilty to joyriding and believed I would only get a slap on the hand. I coordinated my court days for the car theft with a trip to Mexico for more inventory. On the night before the court date my lawyer informed me the probation department had recommended that I serve 90 days. Seems they had me lying about all kinds of things I was not lying about and had me telling the truth about things I was lying about. I had never seen anything so screwed up. There was no time to change things. I would be going to jail.

I served most of my 77 days in a work camp. Marian came to visit every Saturday. I was a model prisoner. I lost a few pounds and got into better shape. It was a freeing feeling, going to jail. It was the opportunity to start a new life. I was paying my past debts off, and in 77 days it would be over and I could start again fresh, with nothing. A lesson learned. Marian and I made wedding plans for when I got out. I was clear that I would never be going back to jail again.

Upon my release, Marian and I rented a small house and set up housekeeping. I got a job working construction. I was a hard worker. In September, 1975, we were married. We honeymooned in Disneyland. We saved our money and worked hard.

We then moved to the same apartment, by the beach, that Eddie had been living in when I visited Father in San Diego. There was a laundromat and a store downstairs, and the rooms that Father and the family had lived in behind the store. Jim Walter owned the building, and I made a deal with him to remodel the apartment.

There was no escalation of violence early on in our marriage. In the beginning, we were the only two in our world. If I did not like something, I got angry and Marian gave in. The same was true in reverse. Marian was taking valium when we first married, then I got mad and she threw them in the toilet and never took them again.

Marian went to the barber shop with me once because she said I did not know how to get a good haircut. She went along and told the barber to keep cutting until there was nothing left on my head. I did not realize it until the next morning. I was pissed but did nothing but stuff my resentment and wear a hat for three weeks.

On the surface, life was good, but underneath, inside me, there was still tremendous fear and anger. I had a need to be recognized, accepted, and understood. I couldn't stand to be wrong. It made me angry to be wrong, angry for needing to be punished for who I was.

One day while having tea, I bumped the kitchen table, and Marian's mom, who was visiting at the time, commented, "Some people sure have awkward children." I felt the fear and anger rise.

I got up, tipped over the table, punched a plant on my way through the living room, then kicked the screen door, almost knocking it off the hinges.

Marian's reaction was one of amusement. I heard her say, "How stupid," as I left. I had always known that I was the wrong man for Marian in her mom's eyes, and this just confirmed that I was wrong, the wrong one. Anytime I felt caught being wrong I exploded and did destructive acts. I blamed Marian's mom for making me so mad because she was from New Zealand and had a very sharp tongue.

I returned later, and Marian's parents were gone. Marian picked up the broken leg from the table and hit me with it. I curled up on the floor, and she kept hitting me. She was as abusive as I was.

I was earning $5.00/hour working construction, and Marian was making practically nothing, so when Father invited us to help him sell plush animals in Las Vegas, we accepted. It was just before Thanksgiving, and this was a good way to earn some quick Christmas cash. Running my father's plush animal stands, we were each able to earn $400 - $500/week.

The pay was excellent, but the friction between Father and Marian was unbearable. Marian tended to tell him what she thought, and he hated anyone who did not agree with him. He tried to use his charm on her, and it would work for short periods of time, but then she would question something and they would not speak to each other for days. All communication went through me, while I tried to please them both. We worked out the season and returned to San Diego at the first opportunity.

I returned to working construction, and we spent our time at home watching TV and making plans for when I got off probation.

After ten months, I convinced my probation officer that we would be better off in Carson, Nevada. I was released from probation, and Marian and I moved. We started out in a rental house that was owned by one of the parents from the Children's Home. I got a job in construction, and Marian worked in a nursing home. It was not long before my construction boss took me aside and explained that I needed to do something that allowed me to expand my horizons. After hours, he taught me to clean carpeting. I took to it like a fish to water. I went home and announced to Marian that I was starting a janitorial service.

Marian and I had lots of good times and some rough times. In a lot of ways, she was like my father. As long as I did what I was supposed to do, things were good. But when I made a mistake, like bumping the table or getting us into business with my father, it was unpleasant.

During the rough times, I would do mean things, from saying things I did not mean, to throwing all her clothes in the yard and causing a huge scene.

As long as I had Marian exclusively, there seemed to be no problems. And the same was true for her. When her family came to visit, I believed they did not like me. For the few days before they arrived in Carson, I was irritable. I wanted Marian to understand how worried I was feeling, and I kept pushing her to talk to me and tell me that everything would be fine when they visited. I could not get satisfaction, and I went nuts, dragged her clothes out in the driveway, and tried to light them on fire. Fortunately, I was not able to get them to burn. I wanted to hurt her like I felt she was hurting me. Her family knew about the incident and felt really bad. They blamed themselves for my problem. After the explosion, I was feeling so bad that it did not matter what her parents thought.

The incidents in Carson seemed to be blamed on her family or mine, and if we avoided them things seemed to be okay. Isolating ourselves from any outside stimulation worked, but of course over time I would want more than just her and she more than just me. It was family connections that threatened us. Her family threatened me, and my family was a threat to her.

Marian was obsessed with cleanliness. If a guest dropped a cigarette ash in an ash tray, she would have it emptied and replaced before the second ash fell. Guests and friends of mine expressed their discomfort with being in our house and preferred us to visit them.

In just nine months, I built a thriving and lucrative janitorial business. I invited my younger brother Al to join me, but that did not last long. Al did not like Marian, and she did not like him. Al and I liked to sit around smoking pot, and when Marian came home, the house would be trashed.

Al had barely left when I decided to expand and invited my brother Eddie to join me. I was on my way to being rich. Marian was very upset with all my actions. I was keeping secrets from her about what I was doing, and she knew it. I could not deal with the feelings of being around her. Emotionally, I was cold, distant, and unavailable. One night she came home from work and threatened me with divorce. The next morning, I called my lawyer and had him draw up the papers. Three days later, we were divorced.

Marian left immediately for San Diego. I was glad to be free of the problems. I was on top of the world. I sold our house and moved into a condo with friends. I kept all the money from the sale, believing I deserved it. I had a new pickup and knew that I was finally successful. I was cool.

Marian returned a couple of weeks later to pick up her belongings at her sister's house. As soon as I heard she was in town, I ran over there and asked her to take a ride with me. I started proving how great I was, and must have convinced her of something, because she stayed. We rented an apartment, remarried, and started over.

I soon found myself deep in debt and blamed Eddie as the problem. I fired him and took over everything myself. In just three months, I was back on top of the world again. I looked at where to expand. I had started helping employees and friends start their own carpet cleaning businesses, and I decided franchising was the answer.

I could tell I was onto something BIG, really big, and I knew that I was in over my head. "So," I thought to myself, "Who is the smartest person I know? Father!" I traveled to Las Vegas, where he was living, and laid out the entire plan. From the first moment I started presenting what I had accomplished and the possible future I saw, Father had suggestions. The logo was not quite right, the equipment was not quite right, and the manual was not quite right, but with his help, we could get this idea ready for a national market.

For the next three months, I drove back and forth between Carson and Las Vegas, a four-hundred mile journey. With Father's guidance, I created a new logo, attempted to invent a new machine, and completely rewrote my manual. I knew Father was smarter than me, and I worshipped getting his approval. Everything I had done in the past couple of years was wrong according to my father, and it felt good having him tell me the "right" way to do things. There was a sense of hope that I would finally get it right, and he was the one I had to prove it to.

Since I had already established four franchises and sold my original operation, I began the project with ample funds. But after three months, cash was running short.

I had more cars, vans, and pickups than I needed, so I sold some of those toys to raise additional funds.

I hocked our house for a small portion of its value. There was no safety net. I had to pay back the loan at a very high interest rate within a short period of time. If I did not pay it back, there would be no foreclosing process, they would own the house no questions asked. I risked everything without any consideration for things not working out. That was not possible and never crossed my mind.

I even borrowed money from my elderly secretary. She invested because of my excitement. Logically, it was a terrible decision, but after listening to me, she mentioned she had $15,000 and was looking for a good investment. Of course, I told her mine was the best, because I believed it to be.

The ads for the franchise were finally in the papers in Phoenix, Denver, and Salt Lake City. We were on our way! Eddie quit his job and joined in the adventure. In Phoenix, we rented a banquet room with a bar and all the amenities. I smelled trouble when only one couple showed up. I had risked everything I had plus things that did not belong to me. Watching Father and Eddie work with the customer, I could see it was not going to sell.

When the client went to the bathroom, I slipped out and stopped him in the hall. I questioned how it was going. He was interested, but he did not like the way he was being pressured. I set his mind at ease and told him I was the owner and president of the company and I would work with him in whatever way made him comfortable.

Inside, I was confused. On one hand, I had put all my trust in Father, and on the other, I could see where we were headed, and I did not trust him. "How could God be wrong?" I wondered. This was the curse, but I believed I could beat it, even if he could not.

I was desperate for cash and made a deal to get a fifteen-hundred dollar down payment from the customer the next day. When I informed Father and Eddie what I had done, Father hit the roof. He explained to me in no uncertain language that he was in charge, and I was the reason for everything that had gone wrong.

He was so angry that we barely spoke from that moment on. I vowed I would not interfere again. I was totally destroyed, realizing that I had betrayed "God." And yet, there was a very small side of me telling me that I was right.

We would continue on to Denver, but he was in charge and hoped he could repair my screw up. In Denver there were only two customers, neither of whom were ready to buy, Salt Lake City was a disaster too. By this time, the old man had given up on anyone buying anything from us, and he was clear: I had done so many things wrong what else could be expected? I had screwed all of us.

Father kept asking, "What did you do with the money?" I did not know what he was talking about. I had just been living and paying for everything. In my mind, I had counted on Father to make this work, and I had done everything he told me to do. For months I had spent money without any consideration for things not working out. I did not overspend, but I went through a large amount of money and had no accounting of where it had gone. All I knew was that we were supposed to be making money by now and that I had not planned on this not working.

In my mind, I was always innocent because the alternative would mean I was guilty and that my father had always been right, I needed to be eliminated. I wasn't innocent, of course. I didn't know what I had spent the money on. Things were not supposed to work out this way. I was unrealistic. That is a pattern in my life, a very big pattern. During the six months that we worked together, I had gone through somewhere in the neighborhood of $60,000.

In Salt Lake City, Father bought a car for him and Eddie to return to Las Vegas in. He was more than angry at me; he was not speaking to me. All communication came through Eddie. Eddie was in trouble himself for buying a diamond ring from a street hustler. The diamond was fake, even though it could cut glass. Father was mad at everyone. Marian was telling me how I did not need them and that we could straighten things out ourselves.

Marian and I started our trek home. We stopped in Elko at one of my franchisee's and spent the night. While there, I got a message from Father through Eddie. I had 24 hours to be in Vegas with the money I owed or suffer the consequences. I called Eddie, and we talked about the fourteen-hundred I had borrowed from him and the thousand I had borrowed from Mom. He said Father wanted a face-to-face meeting with me. I said, "Fine. He will have to come here." A meeting was set for the next morning at 10:00 am in a local casino restaurant. I knew I was in trouble but looked forward to getting it over with.

I asked my friend Tom to accompany me to the restaurant. I also asked Tom to carry a pistol. Tom agreed that if my father tried anything, he would intervene.

I sat with Father and Eddie in a booth. The conversation started off nice enough. Father again asked, "What did you do with the money?"

I started to argue, "What money?" but Father was instantly angry, and I saw his tongue pass over his lower teeth. He was very clear that he was only there to protect Eddie's money, since my screw up had cost him a lot. He said he was not there for himself, but to protect the other people I screwed that did not deserve it, Mom and Eddie.

I said I had nothing, except the van full of equipment. Father demanded that I give Eddie twice his investment in equipment. I immediately agreed, and we went out and unloaded the van. I would have said anything to get this over with. Whatever he said he wanted, I was going to do. All I wanted was to get out of trouble.

I promised myself that I would never, ever have anything to do with either of them again. As a matter of fact, from that moment on, I had no family.

Marian and I returned to Carson. It was time for a disappearing act. We quickly packed and left town. We traveled first to Elko and stayed there a couple of months while I sorted out what had happened. My mistake had been getting under the spell of my father.

We then moved to Bozeman, Montana. It was a beautiful town nestled in the mountains. We rented a nice house and started a new carpet cleaning business. It was just the two of us again, and we got along peacefully.

With the new beginning came a new name. I would return to being called Lee from now on. When we bought the business cards, I said something to the clerk about the future, and he replied that it would not make any difference. I asked him what he meant by his off-hand comment, and he said he would be happy to come to our house and explain. I invited him up for Saturday evening.

On Saturday, Marian and I learned that the world was coming to an end very soon. We could learn about it and how to prepare for it through a group Bob belonged to. It was called the Bahai's under the Covenant. I finally had a purpose in life that made sense! To be right meant everything, and we were the chosen disciples of God.

We sold our new business and spent our time learning how to help the people of the world. We studied, prepared talks, printed books, and started stowing away food. We would be the saviors of the world. The date was set, and we were in the know. During this time, the incidents of violence started occurring more frequently. Anytime I felt threatened or insecure, I would go crazy. It was never my fault. It was always someone else's fault, mostly Marian's.

I had always been jealous of other men looking at Marian. I never blamed the men. It was always her fault. I knew I was the wrong one for Marian, and anytime I was confronted with the thought, I would go crazy and do anything to stop her from hurting me. I felt totally justified in doing whatever it took to stop her.

The first big explosion was when Marian wore her bikini to the dinner table, and a Bahai friend, Mike, mentioned how she was advertising. After he was gone, I started by yelling, then escalated to pushing, and eventually grabbed her by the neck and threw her across the bedroom. I felt justified in my behavior. Earlier in the day she had been lying in the driveway sunbathing, and guys would honk and yell things as they drove by. That pissed me off, and when Mike said he thought she was advertising, I lost it. I waited until after dinner, but then I wanted her to know that what she was doing was WRONG. She did not agree easily.

Although we continued to focus on the world ending, we avoided Mike, and things were pretty much fine. But the undertone was that we both had to be careful not to piss the other off, and we were pretty successful most of the time.

April 29, 1980 came and went as any other day. I had bet everything on the bombs falling. We had two tons of grain, a stockpile of food, and had charged up everything we could with no intention of paying, because the bombs were going to fall. When they didn't, I was again in over my head. We would lose everything.

We had to move. The house we had rented was no longer affordable. "How could I be so stupid?" The words kept ringing in my head. Depressed and frightened, I started looking for work. I found a job helping set up a marketing vehicle for a toilet paper wholesaler who wanted to go to the public with cull paper towels and toilet paper. He was running the business from the basement of a duplex he rented. This was not a real job, it was a get rich quick scheme, but to me it looked like the perfect opportunity.

I spent lots of time with the new company. Soon my boss' wife left him, and I left Marian to join the great adventure. With our separation, Marian moved into a small apartment. The toilet paper gig did not last long. It turned out that the factory supplying the paper products had lots of hot-rod-pink toilet paper, and we could not find anyone to purchase the horrible looking stuff.

With little money and lots of ideas, we bought an old laundromat. Marian borrowed money from her parents to help me get started, and Marian and I moved into a duplex together. Marian was always on my side, no matter what happened.

During this time, we had a fight, and Marian went with her sister to have a drink at a bar. I saw her come out of the bar with a guy, and I ran up and punched him in the nose.

The laundromat only lasted a few months before the lack of funds and success began eating away at the partnership. My partners were so mad at me, I was literally thrown out of the business. I had led them down a rosy path. I did not know anything about being in the laundromat business, as I had led them to believe.

We had also worked on a promotion to raise funds for Big Brothers and Sisters. It was a restaurant 2-for-1 coupon book which turned out to be a disaster. It lacked the quality I had said it would have. The printing was a disaster, and we had to stop selling the book because of disagreements with several different restaurants over the number of books being sold and the number of meals they were giving away 2 for 1. Marian and I moved to Helena, eighty to the west.

Another fresh start, except this time I was a little further down. My brother Al had gotten a settlement from an insurance company and moved to Montana, based on my ideas of ways we could make money. We talked, and I suggested that we form a partnership with a friend of mine and build some fourplexes.

Al came to Helena, and we made a deal for land and put all our ducks in a row to build these buildings. My friend Billy would buy the first one when it was complete. We were about two months into the deal when the interest rates climbed above 13%, leaving us without funding. It was a hard blow to all of us.

We agreed to start a carpet cleaning business together. I did the sales and helped work, and we all made a little bit of money. Al was very unhappy over some money I owed him. It was about twenty-two hundred dollars. One evening, he showed up and demanded that I give him his money or blood. I ended up getting punched a couple of times, and Al got Billy to help him load up everything in the living room, the couch, chair, rocker, and coffee table. He took a sheepskin rug of Marian's that I asked him not to.

I was devastated. I talked to Marian at work, and she came home. The rug was really important to her, and eventually Al agreed to return it.

With nothing left, I went looking for a job that would offer me a future. I found work selling satellite dishes. With only one car, I would work in the mornings, and then Marian would take the car to work in the afternoons. She had gotten a job in a nursing home. From 3:00 in the afternoon until 11:00 at night, I would walk to the store and purchase our food, clean house, cook meals, and spend enormous amounts of time alone. It was the most relaxing, peaceful time of my life. This time I was clear, I would not re-enter the rat race. The luxury of being poor was humbling and enjoyable.

It was not long before I had figured out how to sell satellite dishes. Money was coming in, and we were buying a house. I purchased an old truck and had it painted.

One customer, Vern, had purchased a satellite system from me and soon became my best friend. He would go out and work with me, helping me do demonstrations and installations. Vern had a body shop and was generous to a fault. He always treated me as valuable, and I enjoyed his company. It was not long before I figured out that all these satellite dishes needed a motorized mover that could be controlled from inside the house. One thing led to another, and wham, I was in business building dish movers.

Another customer, Jim, offered to help me with the idea, and we started Satellite Control. I continued with my regular job and worked the Satellite Control business on the side. Marian and I sold our home, and I used half the money to help finance this new venture.

Soon we went to Vegas and introduced our mover at a trade show. The immediate results were slow. While in Vegas, I ran into my brothers. I was walking down the hall in the Riviera Hotel, and there walking toward me were my two brothers. My legs started shaking uncontrollably. I sat down and waited for them to approach. They stopped and said their hellos and goodbyes. "Does the old man know you're here?" Al asked. It had been five years, and I was not up to dealing with Father. I had been told, "Never come to Vegas if you value your life." I was surprised by the strong physical reaction I had to seeing my brothers. Fortunately, I did not see Father or Mom while I was there.

Jim and I returned to Helena and got ready for all the orders to start rolling in. It took about a week to start, but then it was like a freight train. People called wanting to order 10,000 units at a time!

Jim showed up each evening after getting off work from his day job. On the day I had received the call for 10,000 units, he explained to me that we would not be accepting the order. He said the capital to produce them was too high and had various other excuses. He was speaking very strongly for a partner.

I knew that he owned 45%, I owned 45%, and his mother owned 10%. I got mad and told him he could not stop the orders. He explained that I was fired, he owned the whole company, and he would do whatever he wanted. I was beyond mad. I was out of control.

I made a couple of phone calls in the morning and discovered he was right. I owned nothing. I had been duped. I just wanted to move and start over again.

Marian and I moved to Idaho on promises from the owner of a satellite company there that I knew. I took a job opening a new satellite store. I worked my tail off for three months and found that I was grossing less than $800 a month, as well as providing my own truck.

I thought of Vern and decided that he was a good friend and that I would keep him. I had never done that before. Whenever I left a town or area, that was it, nothing worth keeping anyway. Vern was the first person in my life who I decided to keep, no matter what. I called Vern several times and committed to myself that I would keep that friendship.

Marian and I were living on lawn furniture, and she was working in a video rental store with a boss who wanted to get in her pants. Stress was building faster than I could deal with it. I opened a new satellite dish store with a partner and used the leads from the previous job to get us off the ground. I loved working with my partner Bob. He drank too much, but he believed in me and trusted me.

One thing that never bothered me was lying or cheating. When things went wrong, I would do whatever it took to get out of trouble. And this was one of those times.

On the eve of my thirtieth birthday, I had just finished cooking dinner when Marian walked in from a long day at the video store. I immediately sensed she was pissed. She had plenty to be pissed about. Her boss was hitting on her, and her car had been repossessed.

She took one look at me and started talking about what was wrong with me. She even criticized my choice of cooking pots. I did not say a word. I went ahead and served dinner and thought to myself, "I have had it with my life. Thirty years old and still stupid." Somewhere in my mind, something snapped. I knew failure when I was looking it in the eye. Something had to change.

The next morning, I headed off to work on a satellite system for a customer who owned a trade show production company. He was a large fellow with a young pretty wife. He seemed to have all the answers. During the afternoon, while I was finishing the hookup, I mentioned that I was in quite a spot and asked his advice. He asked what the most important thing was to me in my life. I said, "My marriage, but I just can't go on the way we are." He suggested that I check out a "Marriage Encounter." It would clear up any muddy water between Marian and me. That day, I started to live again. I had a mission, and I knew what I wanted. He also offered to sell me a trade show in Bozeman, Montana for ten thousand dollars. I just needed to have a couple thousand down. I called a friend and arranged a loan for the two thousand. I made arrangements to get myself out of business with my partner and managed to "arrange" a little extra profit for myself, as well.

Marian and I moved back to Bozeman. We found a place about thirty miles south of town. I would commute to run the show. But first, we were going to do the Marriage Encounter, then everything would truly be right.

During the Marriage Encounter, Marian was preoccupied with moving. Then, when the grand finale was to happen, Marian fell asleep. That was it. She had not taken seriously how worried about our future I was.

When we arrived in Bozeman, I was watching everything she did looking for evidence to support my belief that our marriage was never going to work. She paid too much attention to her dogs. She was always complaining about how I did things. I saw her as negative angry and cold.

Then to top it all off, her Doberman Pinscher, who was pregnant, was hit and killed by a car in front of our house. This was the last straw for me. I had no compassion for what was happening to Marian. All I could think of was she did not care about me. I withdrew from any connection with her. I would get up each morning adn go to work and stay gone as long as possible.

Finally, one night Marian told me I looked like a pig and she did not want to make love to me. I decided in that instant that I would show her.

There was nothing I could do but leave. But before leaving, I would quit smoking and lose thirty pounds. I was nice to her for the next thirty days. I brought her flowers and was very sweet. Then, when I had lost thirty pounds and been off the cigarettes for six weeks, I dropped the hammer. I was leaving, and there was nothing she could do to stop me. I had collected all the evidence I needed that Marian would never be happy.

I moved into a small apartment and met a beautiful girl named Dawn. It was magical. We always ran into each other. We both had Chevy Luv trucks. She was fun, pretty, and liked me.

It was not long before Dawn and I were making arrangements to live together. She had a six-year-old daughter named Amber. It would be a perfect little family. I did not tell Dawn that I was not divorced yet. That surprise landed like a lead balloon. I did get the divorce. It just took longer than I expected.

During that time, I played many games with Marian. I would call her and convince her how much I cared, and then as soon as she agreed I was worth trusting, I would dump her again. It was a very sick little game I played, but I believed what I was saying each time. Then as soon as I could see we would get back together, I realized nothing had changed and would run away as fast as I could.

This continued even after Marian moved to San Diego. Dawn and I had a fight, and I called Marian and asked her to meet me halfway. We would get things back together. Then Dawn showed up, and I decided that I really wanted her. I was cruel and ruthless in my push and pull with Marian, but this time I burned the bridge. It also created enough damage with Dawn that it was only weeks before she asked me to find my own place.

Since leaving the Children's Home, I had spent fourteen years wrestling with the "curse." I moved 26 times, not counting the army or the time I spent in jail. I lived in 11 different towns. I had 23 jobs.

Like a spinning top, the faster I went, the closer to nowhere I got. I was immature and childish and simply reacted to what life threw at me. I wanted things my way. I was totally acting out with no clear direction or guidance. I was lost and had no way to find my way out.

Under it all was a desperate person willing to do anything to find and fix what was wrong. I was always fixing something: jobs, money, marriage, or place to live, without ever having to confront myself.

Even on the eve of my thirtieth birthday, I committed to "fix" my life. But I was not willing to own any part of the problem. It was about fixing something outside of me. I was not responsible for what was happening in my life, I was only responsible for fixing it. No matter what I did, I could not see the real problem was me.

I could not see that I was the creator of my life. That has been nearly impossible for me to get: that life happens and I choose how I respond. Even if it is a survival instinct that takes over, it is my instinct, and I have to own it. That is really, really hard to own. I have preferred being a victim of my life rather than a cause in my life.

I didn't get that nothing, nothing was ever going to change while I looked everywhere in the world except at myself.

Looking for Love

In April, 1986, at the age of 32, I was still looking for solutions outside of myself. I was looking for someone who would fix my life for me. I thought if someone would love me, everything would fall into place.

Since I was born, I'd had a complaint that nobody wanted me. Nobody loved me. I was nobody's favorite. I had spent my life searching for a particular someone, the person who was glad I was born, the one who would love me and protect me. I was always looking for this person. I had never quit.

Now I thought I had found her in a woman named Jane. I believed she was "the one."

I first saw her that March at the Exchange Club Spring Trade Show. I was with my old partner Billy. He owned the Lumberjack Saloon and periodically bounced in and out of my life. He did not remember her name.

There was something about her that drew me to her, but little did I know how big a part she was to play in the rest of my life.

I had the opportunity to meet her a month later at Timber Expo, a show I was producing for the radio station XT-93. It had been six months since my relationship had ended with Dawn. I had recovered myself and was getting my act together. I was earning good money and investing it all in my trade show production business.

I was also having fun buying and selling used cars for a few extra bucks. The car I drove was always my bankroll. When I needed money, I would sell my car and buy a cheaper one to fix up. Then I would sell that one the next time I needed cash.

When I was producing a show, I was on top of the world. I greeted all the participants with excitement and enthusiasm. I was kind of cocky with confidence. That day, I told the station manager, who was worried about how the show was going, to spend the day golfing and let me do my job.

I met Jane and Yvonne with the same self-assuredness. I first noticed them unloading their pickup before the show. Jane worked for Al's Saw Service in Lolo, and Yvonne was her best friend. They were unloading chain saws, logs, and equipment from the back of the truck. They were attractive women.

Yvonne was the friendly one, but she was married. Jane was quiet and reserved. I flirted with them both as I went about my job.

I stopped in often to check on them. Before they were ready to leave, I invited them up to my apartment, and they accepted. We spent about an hour at my place. Yvonne and I smoked a bowl, and we all laughed and joked together. Yvonne was obvious in her interest in hooking me and Jane up, but she was unsuccessful.

The next morning, I was on the job early and orchestrating a masterpiece. This was truly a talent of mine, like an artist who has a feel for the perfect balance. Unlike other show producers, I spent every minute connecting with the participants. I paid attention to every detail and made sure everything was perfect, from the set of the drapes the night before to the ease of the exhibitors moving in their displays. I personally talked with each booth member and welcomed them and offered to solve any problem they might have.

Jane's booth was in about the center of the show, which was being held in the field house at Montana State University, and the show was on the arena floor. Fifteen feet above the arena, there was a walkway all the way around. I could walk around the entire show with a bird's eye view. Jane stood out from everyone else on the floor. She was wearing a white dress, and every time I looked at her, she was looking at me and smiling.

I did my job from a level I had never experienced before. I was "perfect." By evening, I was making a couple stops an hour by Jane's booth to see if she needed anything. I asked her if after the show that night we could get something to eat together. She agreed, and we stopped at the Burger King, grabbed a couple burgers, and headed for my apartment to relax.

We sat on the floor watching television and holding each other. We eventually made love and fell asleep. It was the easiest thing I had ever done.

The next day, as I was cleaning up after the show, Jane invited me to attend the Loggers Convention in Spokane the following week. During the days between the two events, she said to me, "You can do anything you want." These simple words were like a sign from God to me. These were words I had been waiting for all my life. They gave me permission to be free. All my life I'd had to be careful of what I said or did. I was always looking over my shoulder, waiting for the other shoe to drop. Suddenly, with Jane, that was lifted, and I was free. With those words, I heard that she was the "one" I had been waiting for. She was the one who loved me completely, was glad I was born, and would protect me.

Jane was a tough woman whom I could hide behind. She was the first woman logger in the state of Montana. She worked highway construction, too. She appeared to me to have everything and just wanted to take care of someone. I was no longer responsible for keeping myself out of trouble. I could finally relax. I no longer had to protect myself.

I had never been so moved by anyone in my life. The feelings I was having were strange. I felt invincible, euphoric, unlike I had ever felt before. Her words were like music to my ears. Songs I heard had meaning and spoke directly to my heart. They were popular songs with titles like, "Addicted to Love," "Danger Zone," and "Stuck with You." I was not paying any attention to my fear level. She was "the one."

On Wednesday, we drove to Spokane and stayed in the Sheraton Hotel on the edge of Riverside Park. There was magic in the air. I was living in a world where I was perfect. I was so happy, everyone I met was lit up by being around Jane and me.

Everything about our relationship was a sign from God. We checked into the hotel, and there was a party going on in the banquet room right off the lobby. We were invited in and enjoyed eating from a buffet of hors d'oeuvres. Everything was free, and we were catered to like we were the guests of honor. I never found out what the celebration was. I was so into how perfect I was and Jane was, that I did not know or care what was going on. I enjoyed that everyone saw how special we were.

We ate and retired to our room. We made love and fell asleep. I slept better than I have ever slept. EVER... I was finally safe, happy, whole, and complete.

I awoke in the morning and stood in the window naked, screaming with happiness. I called my brother Eddie before getting dressed. I told him that I had found her, the answer to all my prayers and dreams. No matter how hard I tried to communicate to Eddie how I had found real happiness, it seemed to fall on deaf ears, but he said he was happy for me.

We walked down to the pool for a swim, and then we ate in the restaurant. The food looked and tasted perfect. We went for a walk in the park. There were ducks and geese everywhere. I knocked on the back door of a restaurant near the park and asked for some bread to feed the ducks. They gave me a five-gallon bucket half full of old bread.

We never did make it to the Loggers Convention. We only stayed one night, and time fled by faster than we thought. Throughout the day, I found myself buying flowers and little gifts for Jane. Too soon, it was time to head back home.

It was magical, yet something was out of whack. I started having headaches, which I had never gotten before, and took large amounts of aspirin several times during the day. I was obsessed with Jane, yet she did not look like a goddess to me. She was heavier than I liked. And she was a brunette with green eyes. I liked petite blonds with blue eyes. Something was telling me already that she was not ideal, yet she made me feel so perfect and free that I couldn't see anything beyond my addiction to her. Jane owned a Datsun 280Z sports car and a '79 Ford 4x4 pickup truck. We had taken the sports car to Spokane. I had an older Ford Granada at the time. I was very impressed by her choice in vehicles. Driving her car, I felt "special." Driving nice cars always made me feel special.

We returned to Bozeman, and Jane went back to work. I brought her lunch each day. On the weekend, I met her parents, Helen and Huck. Another sign from God. I had my "ugly" tattoo on my forearm and I always wore long-sleeved shirts to hide it. Somehow, I was so relaxed that I forgot about my arm and met Jane's parents while wearing a short-sleeved t-shirt. When I realized what I had done, I noticed that I felt totally accepted by them.

I was more comfortable in their home than I ever remember being anywhere. They were in their sixties. Huck had trouble walking. He'd had polio when he was eighteen and still wore metal braces on his legs. He was slim and tall, 6'2". He used an old warehouse cart to transport himself anywhere outside the house. He used crutches to get around in the house. He would take the cart to the grocery store or hardware store. Anytime he was outside, he would be on the small gray cart.

In May, Jane and Yvonne helped me with the Bozeman Home and Garden Show. I loved having their help in addition to my regular crew. They both worked greeting people at the entrance.

This was the first time I noticed any sign that things were not perfect with Jane. She was jealous of how I talked and paid attention to Yvonne. She indicated I had hurt her feelings. I was invincible and hardly noticed the rift between us as a problem. After all, I felt perfect.

One of her complaints was that I paid others compliments on their appearance and gave none to her. Thinking back now, I realize that at the time I was not impressed with how Jane looked. It did not matter how she looked. How she made me feel was so much more important than any thoughts I had about how she looked. Yvonne was more attractive to me, but I could not share that with anyone. Jane made me perfect, and I loved being perfect.

At the end of the show, I collected all the items I had taken in trade for space. Jane had first choice at every booth. Then all the people who had helped me received rewards for their hard work. Again, Jane was upset that I was giving things to others. I did not pay any attention other than to notice the conflict and record it.

After the show, I was feeling like a million bucks. There was another show in a couple of weeks in Butte, 100 miles away. I purchased an inventory of leaf jewelry. It was actual leaves dipped in gold. Some were solid and some just the veins. There were also tiny pinecones.

We took Jane's car, the 280Z. We did well financially and had a great time. The idea was mine and so was the money. I assumed Jane enjoyed being with me and wanted or needed nothing. I took her shopping but did not share any of the profit with her. I paid for the motel room, the food, and the fuel.

Jane had a full time job in the saw shop, she had a side business decorating wedding cakes, and her parents were very generous and nice. Upon returning home, Jane was not as happy as I expected her to be, but I could not identify the problem. I just knew something was not perfect in Jane land.

The next show was the Bozeman Collector Car Show and Auction. I was handling the commercial booth displays. I needed to travel to Boise, Idaho to get the equipment for the back draping of the show. Jane's parents and I were getting along as if we had been friends all our lives. I did not own a truck, but Jane did. She agreed we could go pick up the equipment I needed in her truck.

It was not an ordinary pickup. Her truck had custom stripes and wheels. It was a beautiful pickup, and I loved driving it. It made me feel important.

We had been driving all day and were arriving in Boise late. We had stopped along the way to enjoy spring flowers and had made a side trip to explore an old mining dredge. I had booked a room at the Red Lion Motel, and we would stay there before loading the truck the next morning.

As we got close to Boise, I began thinking about the next day. I would be seeing Tony and Doug, from whom I was getting the drapes. Doug also owned the company from which I had purchased the Home Show. They hadn't met Jane before. I was concerned about what they would think of Jane and whether I had done everything right. I was worried about what might go wrong. I wanted them to be impressed. However they judged Jane would be a judgment of me.

I started talking to quell my fears. "This car show is going to be really nice with all the drapes I'm going to do. You know, nobody has ever done a show like this. I'll be the first. This car show is going to really open the door to a whole new line of shows for me." I kept talking and talking and talking, all about me.

"We're going to have a great time producing this show. I think I'll plan more shows for the Mall. You know, your dad and I are talking about my business and the future..."

Suddenly, Jane burst out, "You're just using me, aren't you?"

I responded quickly with "No, of course not!"

"It felt like you were using me in Butte," she said. "I helped you with the show, and you kept all the money."

"So that's what this is about," I fired back. "Money! Well, I thought you just wanted to help me. I didn't know you wanted to be paid!"

"It is not about money," she said. "It's just that you are using my truck and everything is about you."

"I'm paying for everything," I interrupted. "How dare you think I don't treat you fair!" Something inside me snapped. I grabbed my cigarette lighter and threw it out the window. It was like an explosion inside me. I suddenly felt that I was the worst person on the planet. I was in an uncontrollable rage, and I would do anything to stop what I was feeling.

Jane was clearly frightened and surprised.

We drove in silence for a few minutes, my mind trying to process everything that had happened. "Look," I said. "I will divide the money from the Car Show with you."

"It's not about the money," she said. "It's about us sharing things."

"I want to share everything with you," I said, working hard at distancing myself from the explosion. "Everything will be fine, you just wait and see. How about if we go out for a nice dinner?"

"Okay."

"Tomorrow we can go for a nice walk along the river, and then we will load up and go to Sun Valley and visit your aunt and cousins. It will be a great time."

I continued to talk all evening trying to cheer her up and repair the damage I had done. I was totally peaceful and calm, very loving in my eyes. When we arrived at the motel, we were able to eat dinner together and retire to the room.

Something had changed in my burst of rage. It was a huge conflict for me. I had been violent before, with Marian, in trying to stop her from hurting me, but with Dawn there had been no violence. I thought I was free of that kind of behavior, but clearly I was not.

In the morning, we went for a walk by the river. It was nice, but tainted. We enjoyed a beautiful buffet breakfast and traveled to the shop where I rented the equipment. We loaded her pickup and headed for Sun Valley. We stopped there for a visit on the way home.

The magic of our relationship was gone. My explosion had frightened me as much as her. I couldn't remember ever reacting so quickly or having such loss of control. I decided I had to pay better attention, but over the next year there would be many incidences of violence in our relationship.

At the time I would have told you clearly that the violence in our relationship was not my fault. It was a roller coaster ride for me. Looking back I can see that my violence was not just me hitting her. It started with me blaming her for what I was feeling. Then it would escalate, sometimes slowly and sometimes very rapidly. It was always about how she was making me feel. If there was one thing I was clear about, it was not my fault.

The incidences of violence would start over anything. From her not being where she said she was going to be. To catching her visiting with her friends. The one thing that was always true, it started with how I felt in response to what she was doing or not doing. I would always feel bad afterwards, but I truly saw her as responsible for causing my feelings. I would not even consider anything else.

Without warning, Yvonne died. Her husband worked in construction, and they had two small children. She was traveling by herself on a trip to visit relatives and had a single car accident, killing herself. Jane and I attended the funeral, but the tension between us was thick.

Things were changing with Jane. First she would be glad to see me, and then there would be nothing I could do that would please her. Jane was moody, and I was totally controlled by her mood. When she was in a good mood, I was happy. When she was sad, angry, or upset, I was destroyed. The relationship would go from unbelievable ecstasy to the worst imaginable disaster. I was very guarded around her now. I was not "free." Now I was in the relationship for all that it gave me and not wanting to lose anything.

By July, Jane had started spending time away from me. I didn't see or hear from her for a couple of weeks and began living my life as though she would never be a part of it.

Throughout our relationship, the decisions I made based on having Jane around were very different from those I made when I thought she was not going to be a part of my life. An example was hiring my assistant, Debra. I hired her because she was a good salesperson. I had no physical attraction to her, but if I had realized I would be yo-yoing between Jane and no Jane, I would not have hired her. Jane did not like her.

I started making all my decisions from two different mindsets. The first one was with Jane in my life, and the second was based on her not being in my life. The separation between the two was like day and night. In a fight, she had accused me of using her for her vehicles, so I bought a car on payments just to prove to Jane that I could afford anything I wanted.

I was being torn apart by two different parts of me that were at war over whether to be with Jane or not. One part was addicted to her and would do anything to hold on to her. The other part, the one that managed my life, was totally frustrated with the whole situation.

One day, out of the blue, Jane invited me to go horseback riding, and after that things seemed to get better between us. I hung out at her parents' house and helped her dad work on her camp trailer. We fixed it up for her to sell. When the people bought the trailer, Jane's dad suggested that she and I take a little trip on the money. Jane was furious. She disappeared and did not come home for days.

I would stop by and visit her dad every day. We were quickly becoming the best of friends. He was teaching me about the stock market, and I was teaching him about my business.

By August, Jane and I were not speaking again. I ran into my ex-girlfriend, Dawn, at the county fair, and I told her I was not seeing anyone. Jane and I were finished. Two days later, I heard from Jane, and she wanted to talk. Dawn had also called and asked if I would have dinner with her and her daughter. She wanted me to talk to her daughter about some problems they were having.

I hurriedly visited with Jane at her parents' house and returned to my office in time to meet Dawn for dinner. As I was heading upstairs to my office after dinner, Jane came in and asked to speak with me outside. We were standing beside my car when she started asking me where I had been. I lied immediately. Jane started saying things like, "What is that whore doing hanging around here? Are you fucking her?" I kept up with the no, no, no...

My office building was on a major thoroughfare. Suddenly, Jane took a swing at my head, and I blocked her fist. She was caught off balance and fell to the ground.

I helped her up, and she was still very angry. It could not have been five minutes later that we were surrounded by policemen. They approached me and told me they had a witness who had seen me hit her. They frisked me and cuffed me and placed me in the police car.

As we started to drive off, I told the policeman that she had hit me. He explained that the witness saw me hit her. I said, "Ask her. She will tell you that she hit me." He got out and talked to the other officer, and they approached Jane. The next thing I knew, they were putting her in the other police car. The officer said she admitted hitting me, but they had to take us both in because a witness saw me hit her.

We both spent the night in jail. It was not a big deal to me. I had been there before and knew my way around. The next morning, we were taken to the justice court. The judge was a colorful one and near the end of his days in "kangaroo" court, as it was often called.

There were several other prisoners. I was called before Jane. The judge first gave me a lecture about my family history and then said if he were Jane's father he would beat the crap out of me. He asked if I had anything to say, and I said I did not hit her. He said, "How do you plead?"

"Not guilty."

"Fine," he said. "You will be held until we can set up a trial. Or," he went on, "you can plead guilty, and I will give you a small sentence and this will be over."

I said, "Guilty," and he said, "Six months..." My breath stopped, and he continued, "suspended." He told me if I was arrested again for domestic violence, I would serve the six months before any other sentence.

Jane got up in front of him, and he talked about what a good family she came from and how she shouldn't hit people, even if they deserved it. He asked how she pleaded, and she said, "Guilty."

He said, "Six months, suspended." We shared a cab back to my office and agreed that this was not working at all. We each needed to find our own way.

A month later, Jane and I were talking again, and I was again spending time with her parents. Going to jail had had a profound affect on both of us, and our hot, passionate relationship had transformed itself into a peaceful getting along.

Huck and I were talking about the possibilities of working together in the trade show business. We talked about setting up a decorating company to supply all the back drapes at my shows. Our plan was for Jane to run the business.

Huck suggested I go to the bank and borrow operating capital to help my business. Of course, the bank turned me down for a $2,000 loan. I told Huck, and amazingly the bank called me a couple of days later to tell me they had reconsidered my loan and I was approved. I was not stupid, but I also knew better than to argue with a gift horse.

During this time, I purchased Jane an engagement ring. It was simple and not expensive. I talked to Huck about it, and he was excited. When I presented it to Jane, she felt that I was trying to impress her father, and she did not accept my proposal. She was upset and angry that I really did not care about her, only the advantages I could get from her dad.

In October, I ran the Winter Sports Show in the mall. Mall shows are hard to run, and Jane was driving me crazy. I tried to keep her away from the shows now because she was so easily upset with everything I did.

When the Flathead Christmas Show came around in November, Jane was doing anything she could to get my attention. She showed up in Whitefish while I was doing this show. I refused to see her and told her I couldn't be with her while I was working. I felt really bad because she was distraught and clearly very needy. Somewhere in the back of my mind, I kept hoping I would figure this out, but I couldn't let my two worlds collide. In the meantime, I kept busy and focused on my business.

Right after the show in Whitefish, I put together a Christmas Gift Show in Bozeman. Huck had gone into the hospital for surgery. It was supposed to be routine, but after the surgery, he did not recover as he should have. He was in ICU for days, then eventually transferred to a regular room. I was there every day. We sat and talked for hours.

Jane showed up on the second day of the Gift Show and told me how I should be treating her better. I should let her come to the show. I told her I was too busy to be with her, that business was important, and that I had too many problems to deal with. I kept telling her in indirect ways. I was never straight with her. I always blamed it on something or someone else.

The truth was that I couldn't do my job when she was there. I was the one who had the conflict between my world and Jane's. It was impossible for me to make her happy and also take care of myself.

"You don't care about me," she said. "You're keeping me out of your business and your life." She was right, but I was never going to admit it. I was so addicted to her and so desperate to prove I was committed to her.

"If you cared about me, you would let me help you." Part of me wanted desperately to please her, and another part knew that she was bad news for my business. I was so frustrated with not being able to please her, I started punching myself in the face until my whole face was black and blue. I had to hide myself from everyone for the next few days.

The experience of being with Jane was so incredible I was willing to do anything to hold on to it. Just sleeping on the floor in the same room with her was comforting and contented me all the way to my soul. As soon as she would be upset or angry with me, I would become obsessed with doing whatever it took to get her to see that she was wrong.

Whenever I hear that I am wrong, bad, or guilty, my childhood training tells me I must be destroyed. I have a battle going on inside me. If I am not perfect, then I must be destroyed. That battle rages inside me, and I survive by being defensive. I defend being right at all costs because the only alternative is to be destroyed.

Addicted and out of control would be the closest I could come to describing my relationship with Jane. For me, Jane was more pleasing and destructive than heroin. She was alcohol to an alcoholic.

Huck and I were very close. Before he had gone into the hospital, he had fallen in his bathroom. He made Jane and Helen call me, and then he lay on the floor until I could get there to help him. All he wanted was for me to stand there while he got up on his own.

On the day he died, we had been talking a lot about death. One of the conversations was about Jane, and he asked me to take care of her. He was worried about her. I said I would. I was holding his hand as he departed. It was very peaceful. It was a freeing feeling. He was ready to go.

It was only a few minutes later that Jane and her mom arrived. Huck was gone, and their first concern was that someone would steal his wedding ring.

The funeral was planned, and I was not included. At the Autumn Art and Craft Show, I had commissioned a small statue of Huck riding his cart. I had presented it to him just before he went into the hospital. He had loved it. It was cute and said, "Damn, a flat" on a metal tag across the bottom. It looked like him on his cart.

The night before the funeral, I arrived at Jane's parents' house, and Jane said she wanted to talk to me in my car. We started talking about the funeral. Jane informed me that her family would prefer that I not sit with them and that I not be a pallbearer. I exploded uncontrollably with desperation. I started flinging my arms about and yelling, "How can they do this to me?" During this, I hit Jane in the eye. I was devastated and unclear about what to do. My self-hatred took over, and I told Jane how sorry I was. I kept repeating how it was an accident. She believed me and actually appeared to feel sorry for me. She covered up her black eye to protect me from her two brothers who already did not like me or anything about me. They seemed jealous of my relationship with their father and saw me as a con artist.

The funeral was the next day. I sat behind the family. The family put Huck's fishing pole and favorite hat in the casket. They also put his wedding ring back on. I swear his facial expression changed and he seemed to be smiling when the ring was put back on his finger.

After the funeral, I went to the house and was the happy little helper. I did dishes and cleaned up after everyone. Jane's aunt commented to her that I "need to be needed." Later, when Jane told me this, I took it to mean there was something wrong with me. I did not know how she intended it.

After Huck's death, Jane was very busy taking care of her mom and dealing with her dad's affairs. We shared Christmas Day together. Jane gave me a nice wooden dresser for my apartment. Christmas had been a difficult time for me since I was seventeen. This one was no different. I could not relax and enjoy. I felt like a victim and knew that I had a good reason for being upset at Christmas.

I went ahead and purchased the decorating equipment Huck and I had planned on buying to start Royalty Convention Services. It was great, but I no longer had any intention of sharing with Jane. I kept close control and possession of everything.

For Valentine's Day, I bought Jane a pair of earrings and another engagement ring. Then by March, I was hiding from her. In early March, I produced a Home Show in Helena. On the second day of the show, Jane showed up saying she was pregnant. She made a scene, and it was all I could do to get rid of her. I was embarrassed and felt threatened by her presence. She left angry at me, saying I was ruining her life and I was a bastard.

The next day, I bought a new couch at the show for my apartment. When Jane saw it, she got very angry. It was clear to her that I "only cared about myself." That was the truth, but I had no plans for ever revealing it.

It was the push-pull of the batterer. One part of me pulled her closer, and when she got too close, I had to push her away far enough that I felt safe.

The Bozeman Home and Garden Show was the week following Easter. Jane and I had not been speaking since she returned from Helena saying she'd had a miscarriage. I did not believe her. I did not believe I was capable of making babies, so there was always doubt in my mind as to her story. After nine years of marriage to Marian, and no baby, I was sure the problem was me.

My life was pretty much back to normal. I had all my friends who helped me with producing the show. I owned my own decorating equipment and was making more money than I had in the past. The Home and Garden Show was a huge success. On the last day, Jane dropped in, and I found myself bragging to her about how great the show was and how good my life was. I told her that I was going to Vegas in a week to relax and party. Without even a thought, I invited her to join me. She accepted, and bingo, it was a date.

The weather was cool and cloudy in Bozeman when Jane and I boarded the plane. She had never been to Vegas. I was on top of the world. I loved that Jane was interested in meeting my family. I had called ahead and asked Eddie to let us stay at his house. He was more than happy to provide us with a room and a vehicle to use.

We arrived in Las Vegas just before sunset, and Eddie picked us up at the airport. The first thing I asked was how hard it would be to get an eight ball of cocaine. Of course, it was easy. I put up the $250, and we had a great time.

We were like two kids set free in an adult playground. Jane and I were having so much fun being with each other, it was a feeling of euphoria. I was the man, and that was all that mattered.

On Sunday, we visited the hotel where my mom worked as a maid. I had not seen her in fifteen years. I found the head of housekeeping and asked to see her. We met for maybe five minutes in the stairwell of the hotel, and I introduced her to Jane. Somehow I felt it was a very big deal that I had introduced her to my mom. We only chitchatted about the weather and that we were going home on Tuesday. No one appeared comfortable.

On Monday morning, we got up and headed for breakfast at the Circus Circus buffet. It had been the perfect weekend. No fighting, no upsets, nothing but perfection. We were driving Eddie's old Chevy pickup. We had to roll down the window and open the driver's door from the outside. We valet parked. As we exited the truck, Jane pointed to a small wedding chapel across the street and said, "I dare you to go over there and marry me!"

I laughed and thought, "I'm not afraid of no piece of paper." To me, that was all marriage was, a piece of paper. When I divorced Marian I had proven that I was really in control and could control the outcome of anything if I really wanted to. I was not worried about a piece of paper. As long as things were fun, I would enjoy them, and if they did not work out, I was confident that I could get out of anything.

We went in to Circus Circus and feasted on the huge buffet. After breakfast, we walked across the street and entered the wedding chapel. We had run out of cocaine on Sunday morning, but the high of just being with Jane made cocaine like children's aspirin to me.

It was May 4, 1987 when we tied the knot in Vegas. The next morning, we flew back to Bozeman. On the way to the airport, Eddie offered us his advice about marriage, "Don't ever go to sleep with unsettled anger." I called Debra in my office and told her of our marriage and that I would be taking an extra day off.

I lived in a small apartment in the Harvest Creek area. We arrived there in late afternoon. The sun was shining, and the air was fresh. I remember the surprise when we walked in the door. In the dining room, hanging from the light fixture, were paper wedding bells. There were silver and white balloons tied to the back of one of the kitchen chairs. On the table were two champagne glasses, a bottle of Cold Duck, and a small wedding cake. Between the glasses and the Cold Duck was a large white envelope.

I was amazed and surprised. Jane was wearing her cowboy boots, the red ones with the little wing tip. She picked up the card from the table and opened it quickly. As she read, I was thinking what a wonderful thing Debra had done.

Suddenly, Jane reached over and pushed the cake off the table. Before it could hit the floor, she dropkicked it over the back of the couch. I froze in shock. Jane handed me the card and said, "That bitch is in love with you." I looked at the card and saw it was signed, "Love, Deb." As Jane stomped out of the house, she yelled, "I can't believe you chose her over me."

It was several days before I heard from Jane. I returned to work and pretended that everything was fine. Within a week, I talked to Jane, and she told me she was going to Texas to attend a travel agent school so she could get a job. I contacted my attorney, a shyster and an opportunist, and shared with him the incredible mistake I had made. I told him, "Just get me out of this. I don't care what it costs."

"With your luck," he said, "she's probably pregnant." I laughed, and he said, "Let's wait thirty days and see, because if she is, you will want to be involved in the baby's life." We talked for awhile, and I agreed to wait a month and see. I was not too worried. We had only been unprotected once, on the night of our wedding.

It was shortly after the first of June that Jane announced she was pregnant. She was living at home and would soon be leaving for Texas. I made up my mind that I was going to be a father and husband, no matter what.

For the next month, while Jane was in Texas, we talked every night, sometimes for hours. I was studying everything I could find about relationships. The last week before her arrival home, I made poster board signs. They were all on a white background and were painted with poster paint in a variety of colors. Some were decorated with hearts and others with smiling faces. All had inspirational and loving sayings like, "I Love You," "You are the light in my life," and, "I love Jane." There were 10 signs, and they were on the walls and ceiling of the bedroom. Then in the living room, there were smaller signs with more sayings of inspiration and love.

I picked her up at the airport on the last day of June. We swung by her parents' house to pick up her car. We met at my apartment and got settled in. I was walking on eggshells.

Jane opened the refrigerator and said, "Why haven't you bought any groceries?" Her voice was sharp and piercing. I panicked.

"Well..." I stuttered.

She started yelling, "You don't really care about this baby do you? What kind of father won't buy food for his family? You really don't want me in your life." She stomped out of the house and slammed the door behind her.

The Fourth of July weekend arrived. I was depressed to the point of suicide. I was not eating, and Debra invited me to join her family at Flathead Lake for the weekend. I agreed to go. It was better than sitting home.

Jane and I had agreed to see a marriage counselor. It only lasted three meetings before Jane refused to return. He was not the "right" counselor.

We started seeing a peer counselor at "The Women's Place." It only lasted a few visits before Jane was convinced that I was conning the counselor. I did not think much of the "peer counselor" because it seemed that she was more concerned about her anger than ours.

I was so depressed, I could not think clearly about anything. My business was going broke quickly. Sometimes I would not show up for work for days. Then the days turned into weeks, and one day I realized that I needed to sell my business.

By the first of August, I had sold my business to Deb. I basically gave it to her to pay off the debts I owed. I traded the convention service company to my friend Horton. He gave me four acres of land that I was able to borrow money against from the bank.

Jane and I had a pattern of getting along for anywhere from a few hours to, on rare occasions, a few days. When we got together, it always had the same result. There would be extreme passion at first, and it would generally end in violence. Most of the time it was me exploding because she would point out where I was wrong or lacking. I would try to control her for a different outcome, and she would try to punish me for hurting her.

My view was that I was completely innocent. It was her making me feel out of control, and I could not help what was happening to me. I considered myself to be like an abused dog. If you scare him, he will bite you, and it is not the dog's fault. You should know how to behave in the presence of an abused animal. Jane should have known how to behave around me. It was obvious I had been hurt, and if you threaten an abused dog, you will get bitten. That's all there was to it.

I was addicted to her. I would be "sober" sometimes for weeks, then I would see her, and bingo, I would be overwhelmed with wanting her again. I felt cursed by some evil power outside of me.

I attended one doctor visit with Jane, and the doctor informed me that I was dangerous, I had to leave her office, and I was not welcome at any further visits. I was devastated that Jane had told the doctor enough on previous visits that she had asked me to leave.

The county fair was coming up. I purchased a booth in the fair and set up a golf putting game. It was a disaster, but it kept Jane and me busy for several days. We got an appointment with the Mental Health Center. This time it only took two visits before the counselor was not going to be able to help us, according to Jane.

Now I was going crazy. One minute it looked like everything was going to work out, then the next it was the end forever. I was desperate for an answer. When I would decide that I needed to talk to Jane, I would hunt her down, and the results were always the same. I was desperate for her to understand me, and she was not interested in fixing my desperation.

One time I found her at her favorite saloon. She did not drink, but just hung out there and visited with friends. I came in, and she was sitting alone. I tried to act like I had not hunted her down.

I walked up and started a friendly conversation. Then I started pushing for an answer. "What are we going to do?" The harder I pushed, the more she resisted. Things escalated, and I followed her to her car. By this time, I was apologizing in one breath and begging in the next.

"Anything, just give me anything," I pleaded as she started the car. I held the door open, continuing to verbally push. She backed the car up, and I hoped I would be hurt. That would stop the craziness, I knew.

I even tried to act like I was hurt, but nothing was working. Jane drove away. I looked around to see if anyone had seen me. The coast was clear, and I got into my car and went home. I had no desire to go anywhere or do anything.

After a couple of days, I decided that the only way out of this mess was to end my life. As I thought about it, I realized what a waste my life was. I pulled my car into the garage and raised the hood. It would look like an accident. I let the car sit running for twenty to thirty minutes at a time. I removed a spark plug and put it back in. I left the door open to the apartment until I was sure the house was also filled with carbon monoxide.

At about 4:00 in the afternoon, I laid down on the couch and drifted off to sleep. My head was aching. I knew the end was near, and I felt relieved.

I had barely closed my eyes when the front door burst open and in walked Jane. I asked, "What are you doing here?"

She replied, "I was driving to Belgrade and suddenly knew I had to come up here." She opened the doors and windows and then helped me into her car. She drove me to the hospital. Lying there in the emergency room, I knew this was another sign from God. There was something more for me to do. This was clearly an intervention by a power greater, much greater, than I. Jane had been driving in the opposite direction from my apartment and suddenly turned around and drove there in time to save my life.

The doctors put me on oxygen and told me how lucky I was. The carbon monoxide levels in my body were so high they were surprised I had not suffered brain damage. I stuck to my story about an accident. Nobody believed me, but I did not care.

Jane and I agreed to try and work things out, but three days later there was the regular explosion and her saying I cared more about making money than I did about her.

Over the years, a number of times I had sought out the advice of a trance medium. She channeled a group of spirits called "Amog." Each time I sought their advice, it was interesting and mystical. This time I had a clear purpose in what I wanted to know. "Why can't Jane and I get it together or keep it apart?"

They told me the following story. A long time ago, in the Victorian age, we were brother and sister. We lived in a large family, and we were very close. Our mother was meek and our father very dominating. While growing up, Jane and I had played together and always pretended that we were the only two people on the planet. We were very close and fantasized about being husband and wife.

Of course that was totally unacceptable, and we went our own ways, but always believing that if we had been allowed to be together, we would have had a happy and fulfilling life. So we had come together in this life to complete the past and see that happiness in life was not the result of being with the right person. It took me years afterwards to understand how true this was.

Like an alcoholic wanting a drink, I was sure I would never go back to Jane, and I did not want to go back. With this new information, it was much easier for me to stay away from her. I had an answer that explained why I was so crazy about her and also why we could never be happy together in this life.

I worked at earning money. I purchased a new car and starting feeling really good about myself. Then, in mid-September, I began to obsess about Jane and being a family. I again started hunting her down.

It took a couple of days, but I found her at her friend Leah's house in Belgrade. My mind had gone crazy the past couple of days looking for her. I had considered every negative thought imaginable.

Often times, I would think she was with another man. That was the highest threat I could feel. It would confirm how bad I was. And if I were "that bad," I would have to do something to end my life.

I had always fought the idea that I was really bad because its acceptance would also mean accepting the punishment that went along with it. The ultimate punishment was death.

These thoughts always ran in the back of my mind. After attempting suicide and failing, I believed there was some grand purpose to my life, but every time I became obsessed with Jane, my need for approval and acceptance overrode everything else. I knew if she would just talk to me, this time I would get it right. And everything would work out.

I arrived at Leah's house and asked to talk to Jane. She was six months pregnant. I asked her to go for a ride with me. I was talking very fast. This time I was sure I had the answer, if she would just listen.

I grabbed her arm and started pulling her toward my car, which I had parked 25 feet away. I pulled her 15 to 20 feet before she sat down and was going no further. She was screaming at the top of her lungs. I was completely obsessed with getting her to listen to me when suddenly I realized I was in serious trouble. Jane's friend was yelling at me that she had called the police. I started telling Jane I was sorry, but it was too late. I ran around my car, got in, and drove off.

I could not believe what had just happened. Now I had to figure out how to fix this new problem. I headed straight for home. I would hide out until this blew over. I did not know what to do.

The next morning, the sheriff served me with a restraining order, and it was over.

I had started seeing a counselor at the Mental Health Center a couple of months before. I never told her what happened. I went there to proclaim my innocence and protest the treatment I received by an unjust life.

It was very clear to me that Jane and I were finished forever. I had finally burned enough of the bridge that I would never be going back. I worked at my newest venture, an enterprise called Finders. We found anything that people were looking for. I enjoyed the support and love of my friends, none of whom knew

Jane. I spent my off hours alone smoking pot and pretending that everything would be all right. I often toyed with the idea of killing myself. It was reassuring that I could stop the pain if necessary, but I would hang on for one more day and see what happened. Each time I would accept that death was a real option, the pain would subside, and I would feel relief from the pain of being so bad.

My birthday came, and I told no one. It was too painful to think about celebrating the birth of a person so bad. Christmas came, and I hid out in my apartment and avoided all the parties. With the aid of marijuana, I was able to survive and appear to be normal in public.

The Beginning of the End

It was January, and I had not spoken to Jane since trying to force her into my car the previous September. I had a restraining order against me and the certainty of a six-month jail sentence should I ever be convicted of domestic violence again. I was still operating Finders and trying to pick up the pieces of my life.

The receptionist poked her head in my office door. "It's your wife. She's at the hospital and about to give birth. She wants you to come immediately."

"WHAT?" My mind spun as I looked at Debbie. "What?! What are you talking about?" I was stuttering with shock. "You know she has a restraining order against me."

Debbie smiled. "It's all clear for you," she said, "so go see your baby being born."

I drove across town in disbelief. Each stoplight offered new thoughts to contemplate. "Maybe she is setting me up. Ah ha, that's it. She just wants to put me in jail." Then by the next stoplight, "No, she really loves me! That's it." It was at least five miles across town, and every stoplight seemed to be red.

Suddenly, I was pulling into the parking lot of Community Hospital. My blood was pumping. As I got out of the car, I reached over and grabbed my box of cassette tapes. We would need music.

The smell of hospitals had always bothered me, but today there was no smell, just light and smiling faces. As I approached the nurse's station, I felt totally confident. After all, I was the father. I could see in the nurses' faces they had heard I liked to hit my wife, but I felt immune to their thoughts and beliefs. I was walking so tall I was sure my feet were not even touching the floor. At the nurse's station I was told Jane was in the birthing room, just down the hallway. I strode down the hall and opened the door.

The first thing I saw was Jane lying on the bed. Her smile told me everything was okay. I looked around the room. There were just the two of us. The room was painted a light pink and trimmed in white. The lights were soft, and there were friendly pictures on the walls. I recognized the sweet smell of Jane in the air. She was so happy to see me. She gave me her "little girl" smile, the one that says, "I need you, you are my hero, and I love you."

I went to the nurse's station and asked for a cassette player. I was in the "zone." Everything I touched turned to gold. Everything was perfect, and I was orchestrating it all with perfection. I set up the tape player and inserted a George Winston tape, "Winter." The sound of the piano, delicately filling the air, brought peace, happiness, and wonder to the room.

Kathy, Jane's coach, arrived right on schedule. For the next hour and a half, I held the hand of the woman I loved. Even with all the excitement, there was a sense of calmness in my heart, a confident and peaceful feeling that reached into the depths of my soul. The smells and the sounds were all dancing like a whirlwind in the air. Then, in a single moment, everything stood still.

I was there, but somehow I was not. I could see the top of a head, a face, shoulders, and poof, a whole and complete baby. The doctor handed me scissors and showed me where to cut. She was beautiful, the most beautiful thing I had ever seen. I walked over and set her in Jane's arms.

Since conception, the baby had never been real to me. It was something inside Jane. Now, instantly she was real. I touched her, heard her, saw her, smelled her. She was real. And I was in shock and bewildered by the whole ordeal. How something so precious could come from anything I did was beyond me. I stepped back and took a deep breath. As the air rushed from my lungs, I relaxed.

The hospital served a special dinner for us as the new, proud parents. We had lots of visitors and lots of love. Best of all, I was there. Jane needed me. Our daughter needed me, and so did Jane's mom. It was a miracle. My "someday" had just arrived. I felt whole, complete, with an appreciation for being in the right place at the right time. The hospital gave me a special little card with our daughter, Jennifer's, footprints on it, evidence that I was the father. And a proud father I was!

We left the hospital and stayed at Jane's mom's house. As each day passed, my natural fathering seemed to take on a life of its own. I was the perfect caregiver, waiting on everyone hand and foot. I had found my calling. Cooking, cleaning, doing laundry, babysitting, and parenting, I was great at them all. There was not an angry bone in my body. I was grateful and obedient.

I was there ten days before it all came crashing down around me. I was sitting in the living room rocking Jennifer, while my mother-in-law sat across from me eating lunch. Without warning, the front door burst open, and in walked Jane. She was wearing her wingtip cowboy boots, and her walk was more of a stomp. She crossed the room and snatched Jennifer from my arms. "GET OUT," she ordered.

"What?" I said, half stuttering. "WHAT! You want me to leave? You have got to be kidding!" I could hardly breathe.

She repeated the order, a little louder. "GET OUT NOW!"

In the background, I could hear her mom saying, "Jane, Jane, Jane." She kept repeating her name over and over. Jane was not hearing her.

I had been the perfect father, the perfect caregiver, and I asked for nothing in return. After ten days of happiness, peace, and celebration, I could not believe it was over.

"You haven't changed," she said. "Get out now and don't ever come back." The shock of her anger was instantly sobering. I hurriedly tried to gather up what I could of my belongings. Jane set the baby in the swing and started pushing me toward the door. "If you don't get out now, I'm calling the police," she said.

"What? What have I done?" I asked, backing out the door.

"You bastard, you will never see Jennifer again." The door slammed behind me.

As I drove home to my apartment, I began to cry. First, gentle flowing tears danced on my cheeks as they worked their way to my neck. Then the dam burst, and the sobbing began, stirring old, very old, emotions from deep within my gut. I had been perfect for the past ten days, and now I was the devil himself.

I was 34 years old, and I had just witnessed the birth of my only child. For the first time in my life, I was experiencing love at a level that had never existed for me. The love I felt for my daughter took my breath away.

"I am innocent!" I screamed as I pulled into my driveway. My dad had always flipped out and punished whoever was to blame. Then there was Marian, who was angry and sharp with me. Nice thing with Marian, I could stop her. Now here I was married to Jane, and she flipped out. I couldn't figure out why, and I couldn't stop her without going to jail.

I was screwed again by life.

My apartment was quiet. I grabbed myself a soda pop and rolled a joint. My body was numb. My mind was stretched so tight that it no longer could function. Sitting on the couch smoking a joint and sipping from my Mountain Dew, it was only a few minutes before I left it all behind. I felt good again, relaxed and at peace with the world.

I awoke in the morning to find the sun shining in through the dining room window. I had slept on the couch. What to do with myself? Ten days ago, I had walked away from work, my friends, and my life to join Jane. Should I call her? The restraining order was still in place. Jail was just a phone call away. Oh, but the baby, what a beautiful baby! I resolved to get up, go to work, and keep busy.

I had taken on the management of my office building. It was a new cooperative office complex having about 60 different businesses. There were stockbrokers, counselors, massage therapists, a dating service, and on and on. I handled all aspects of managing the property and was in charge of completing construction for the last half of the building. I had a small office and a small income. I considered myself to be the "anything for a buck" man.

I had one business idea after another, a continual roller coaster of starts and stops. Nothing was successful. One was the "Senior Care" program, a plan that raised money and funded programs to cure the loneliness of senior citizens. Jane lived with her mom, who I loved. She always treated me special, and I had seen much loneliness in her eyes. I thought perhaps this was how I would change the world.

No matter how hard I tried with each new venture, something always went wrong. The funds did not start flowing in, and I found myself in financial trouble. The income created from managing the office building was not even paying my apartment rent, let alone my car payment or other bills. Here I was in trouble again. As far as child support, the state accepted my financial excuses and only required me to pay $50 per month. I knew I had to do something and do it fast. Carpet cleaning had always worked before. It would work again. With a little borrowed money, I picked up some used equipment and an old van. Soon Showcase Carpet Care was born. For the next three months, I focused on getting new accounts and doing the work. I worked around the clock. No job was too big or too small for me. All along the way, I was reminded why I had given up this business in the past. It was hard work and physically demanding. Every day, I felt a little better about myself and my world. Again in control, I had pulled myself up and out of immediate danger. Again, it was time for a change. The divorce was moving along slowly. I was tired of working so hard, so I placed an ad in the newspaper listing the business for sale. Within days, I had several people interested in owning their own business. I priced it right, and, bingo, it was sold within two weeks. With a new bankroll, I was on my way again.

Jane had moved from her mother's house to her own apartment. I sent her cards and called her occasionally. One thing led to another and soon we were talking.

I visited her at work and hung out. She was baking and making sandwiches for the Basket Lady. The Basket Lady traveled around from business to business selling her basket full of treats and sandwiches. Jane worked in the basement of the Basket Lady's home making and preparing all the food.

Things started out innocently enough, with me seeing Jennifer, who was now six months old, and visiting with Jane. When things started to get a little uptight, I would leave. Simple enough. We would just see each other for the sake of Jennifer.

Soon we were seeing each other daily. I was pursuing another new adventure, freelance loan brokering. My pocket was full of money, and all the fires were out.

I did not tell any of my friends I was seeing Jane, and I would lie if asked. Nobody supported me seeing Jane. I was afraid they would tell me how crazy I was. More than that, I was afraid they would stop me because they didn't know how violent I might get while thinking I was defending myself from Jane.

I didn't tell Jane about my friends, either. She always exploded when I talked about work or friends. She would use whatever I said to prove that I really did not care for her. She would call my friends nasty names like, "that bitch," or "asshole." She hated my friends and my work.

It was important to keep my worlds separated at all times. Both worlds had their own secrets, and as long as I kept the secrets hidden, both worlds would be safe. I didn't stop to ask where I was in all this. Juggling two worlds was automatic for me. It was an effortless task.

One day, after several of these visits, Jane and I went back to her apartment after work. On the way, we stopped to browse at a yard sale. Talking with the people there had an effect on me, and I spoke as if we were a happily married couple. I used the term "we" quite a bit. We did not buy anything, but something in the conversation made me feel like there was a future.

On the way home, Jane was quiet and withdrawn. I could feel there was something wrong. As we climbed the stairs to her apartment, I asked myself what was going on. We had just begun speaking again, and I loved seeing Jennifer, holding her, being her dad. This was important to me.

Her apartment was kind of messy, like she had never unpacked from moving in or that she was only there temporarily. Jennifer was asleep, and Jane set her in the crib in the living room. I asked, "Why are you mad at me?"

Jane responded, "You liar! You don't want to be with me. You don't want to live with us. You won't even support your own daughter."

"You abandoned us. Your friends are more important than we are. All you care about is yourself."

I couldn't think. So what if I had lied. I lie all the time. Everyone lies. I didn't mean to make her mad. Panic filled my entire being. Inside I screamed, "I am innocent!" I was completely overwhelmed with fear. I had to stop her from saying all those nasty things.

"I love you and Jennifer," I said.

"You don't love anyone but yourself."

Inside my mind I was screaming, "STOP, STOP, STOP." Before I knew it, I had grabbed her arm. As she resisted, I pushed her to the couch. She was screaming at me. I thought to myself, "I know I am in control." She was out of control. I knew what I was doing. With each decision to increase the amount of pressure holding her down, I knew that I was in control. Deep inside my being, I screamed to myself, "Can't you see how much you are hurting me? If I really wanted to hurt you, I could. I am only stopping you from hurting me."

She broke free of my hold. "You bastard, you can't touch me," she said and walked off into the bedroom.

"Jane, I'm sorry," I said. "I didn't mean to push you. I'm sorry." By this time, Jennifer was awake and crying. I approached the crib and picked her up. Jane returned from the bedroom and took Jennifer from my arms.

"Get out," she said. "Get out now."

I wanted desperately to stop her from hurting me with her words, but nothing came out of my mouth.

With Jennifer in one arm, she was crying and screaming at the top of her voice, "Get out. You don't care about us." I could see there was no hope of stopping her. It was too late. I grabbed my coat and ran from her apartment, her words bouncing off my back. "You will never see this baby again!"

From the parking lot, I yelled, "Jane, Jane." She came to the window, and I yelled, "Please don't do this."

She opened the window and yelled back, "If you don't leave, I am calling the police." Scared, confused, and disillusioned, I started my car.

The words, "Jane is nuts, Jane is nuts, Jane is nuts!" kept echoing through my mind on the drive home. I couldn't believe how out of control things had gotten. I remembered how mad my dad would get when he caught me doing something wrong. Was I stupid or what? I could not understand how one moment someone could think I was so nice and the next moment I would be the devil himself. It made no sense. Why was she in my life? Why did she act exactly like my father? The questions were overwhelming. The only thing to do was go home, get stoned, and escape all the chatter between my ears. Tomorrow would be better.

Morning came much too fast. Smoking pot, eating, and watching TV always had a price to pay in the morning.

I got up early and got myself going. I had a lot to do. Today was special. Today, I would seek employment. Yes, a real job.

I was amazed how easily I was hired. District Sales Manager. What a title. What a job! It was straight commission but with loads of potential. That was all I needed to get started, someone who believed in me and something to sell. We were marketing a new device. It was a surge suppresser, and when installed in a commercial business, especially one with a high electric bill, it would pay for itself in a very short time.

The selling was easy for me. I never questioned whether it worked or not. I believed my boss when he said how well it worked. Besides, there was a total money-back satisfaction guarantee.

Within 90 days, all my bills were again current, and I was on my way to a very successful career. The sweet smell of success. It was a beautiful morning as I sat at my desk daydreaming about my future. I idly watched the people strolling up and down the sidewalk, smiling and happy.

The mail was lying on the corner of my desk. The first envelope contained an offer for a chance to win a million dollars. I tossed it in the round file. The second envelope was from my boss. I was the top salesman in the company. With excitement and anticipation, I opened the letter. As I read it, I couldn't believe my eyes. Going out of business? How could that be?

I had been led down a rosy path. But even more importantly, I had led a number of local business owners down that same rosy path. The guarantee was not worth the paper it was written on. Another bad deal. Of course, none of it was my fault, yet feelings of shame and embarrassment flooded my entire being. I thought about all the people I had sold this bill of goods to. I was sure they would be very disappointed in me. I imagined their anger. But it wasn't my fault! My dad was not right. I was not dumber than a box of rocks.

I resisted that thought with every ounce of energy I had. I was not stupid. It was not my fault. It was the curse. Life just seemed to keep screwing me over and over and over.

It had been months since I had spoken with Jane. I felt lost and confused. I wanted to see Jennifer. I felt like I was again at a crossroads where I had been too many times, and each time the scene was the same. I was somewhere I didn't want to be with no idea of how I got there.

I joined a Friday night ACOD group, Adult Children Of Dysfunction, a 12-step group working a modified version of the AA 12-step program. Knowing that I needed help, this seemed like a simple enough approach. I had first started private counseling when I left Marian five years ago, and now I was a pro at fixing myself. I had always known I was smarter than the counselors, and besides, I knew better than to trust them with my secrets. Hell, I had secrets I didn't even trust myself with. These meetings were easy to attend, and they brought a sense of belonging and comfort to me.

The group was made up of about half men and half women.

I had promised myself that I would not get seriously involved with anyone until I could figure out how I had gotten into the mess I was in with Jane. So, I was open to exploring pure friendship with women, and Jan, one of the other participants, offered me the opportunity.

My relationships with persons of the opposite sex had always been about fulfilling some sort of agenda. Bottom line was it had to do with sex. I thought if a woman liked me, that meant there were roles that each of us must play. I had never been friends with a woman without heading in the direction of sex, commitment, and making myself feel good. But this time it would be different. I knew it was in the relationship with women that I ended up getting totally screwed with no understanding of what had gone wrong. Now the question in my mind was, "If I can't control women, can I control myself?"

After one of the ACOD meetings, a number of us went to have coffee at a small café next door to the meeting room. Jan was clearly interested in me. Here I was, with someone who could make me feel good, and I knew it would not last. I wanted to prove to myself that I could control me. As the evening went on, I flirted, I was funny, and I was entertaining. I walked Jan back to her car. What a wonderful evening! The sense of being desirable filled my body. The idea that I was in control again brought it all together.

The 12-step stuff was working its magic. Everything in my life was coming back together. I was spending a little time each weekend with Jennifer. She was so cute, innocent, and vulnerable. I was still arranging financing for hard-to-get loans. I was paid a finders' fee by clients, and things were looking up.

I was still constantly broke and barely able to pay my bills. Bob, the owner of the building I was managing, offered to finance me buying cars and driving them to Las Vegas where I would sell them and make money for both of us. I had seen it done a number of times. My older brother, Eddie, had even hired me several times to do the driving in the past.

It was not long before I came up with an improvement on the perfect plan. I would purchase two pickups, load them with Christmas trees, and drive one and tow one to Las Vegas. When in Vegas, I would sell the trucks and the trees. It was perfect.

I knew what to do and started shopping. I had a five thousand dollar budget. The first pickup was an easy purchase. It was a '74 Ford with some body damage, but a good runner and would be a quick seller in Vegas. The next one had to be exceptional. I spotted a '72 Chevy, custom cab, long-box with air. The air was important for bringing in the big money in Vegas. I purchased the truck for $400. Sure, it needed work, but at the purchase price, how could I go wrong? When done, this truck would bring four to five thousand dollars in Vegas. I took the truck to my friend, Willy, the mechanic, who worked out of his garage at home. It was perfect. Everything was perfect. I was on a project that was new and exciting.

The best deals for fresh-cut Christmas trees were on the Indian reservation. I placed an order for enough trees to fill both pickups. Every couple of days, I checked with Willy about the progress of my truck. There seemed to be a different issue every time I stopped in. First, it was the carburetor, then the distributor, then the valves needed adjusting. On two occasions, I picked it up and did not make it three blocks before something else went wrong. What I had thought were some minor repairs had turned into a three-week ordeal. It was as if the truck were jinxed. Everything else was still on target. I would just have to pick up the trees and store them in my yard. I told myself that nothing ever goes as planned.

I had shopped around for a body shop that would give me a "deal." A father/son team of Frank and Jerry were perfect. They said they could straighten the frame and make the truck look like new for only $600. I would have to wait until they could get to it, but they would hurry once it was in their shop. This was fine. I still needed to get the interior done.

I was finally able to get the truck to drive across town without a new problem showing up. I drove it to the upholstery shop, and they started their magic. It got a new carpet, new seat covers, and a new pad on the dashboard. This was going to be one nice truck. It only took the upholsterer a week to get it done. I picked it up on Friday and took it directly to the body shop.

The trees were ready, so I traveled up to the reservation with the Ford pulling a trailer. I loaded and hauled all the trees down and stored them in my yard. It was only a few days until I would be ready to leave. Toward the end of the week, I stopped by the body shop, where Frank explained that the damage to the truck was much worse than he had anticipated. He would have to change the entire frame. He would do it for the same money, but it would take longer.

The following week, I stopped again to check on the truck. The door was locked. I thought it was strange that a business would have their door locked during the middle of the week. Suspicious, I looked around and realized that there were no vehicles in the parking lot. My mind raced. I called the junkyard shop that had recommended Frank to me. Harold explained that Frank had some problems and had moved home to Livingston, two hundred fifty miles away. I asked if he knew where my truck was, and he said that he would have Frank call me.

It was a couple of days before Frank called. He explained that the truck was in good hands. He had taken it with him and would get the work done and bring it to me, but it would be Christmas before it could be done. My heart sank. What would I do with a yard full of Christmas trees? Funds running low, I had made myself a small loan from the bankroll Bob had provided, and things were not looking good for going to Vegas.

Dick, one of the guys in the office building, suggested that I set up a Christmas tree lot locally to sell the trees and earn a little money. I got busy and rented a location. He offered his help, and we borrowed a travel trailer for an office. We worked together and split the profit.

We did everything we could to sell those trees. Dick went out every couple days cutting new trees, and our lot looked great. We didn't have the really nice trees. Ours were the same ones anyone could cut locally. They would have been great in Las Vegas. The demand in Bozeman was not there. We worked 12 hours a day for 30 days. At the end we had $600 profit to split. That was a net earning of $10 a day. The big question, though, was what I was going to do with 300 leftover trees. It was amazing to see them spread around the perimeter of my yard.

Christmas was just like all the ones from the past. I seemed to have few friends. I struggled with missing Jennifer, wanting to experience the excitement of watching her open presents. Thank God for pot. At least I could get stoned. It was a long, cold winter with a yard full of Christmas trees.

As spring approached, I found my connection with others began to increase. I saw Jennifer every week. I had sold one truck. Finding funding for projects helped pay the bills. I still managed the office building and had enough money to survive. Court dates with Jane kept being postponed. We had started talking again, first just innocently, then it grew. We were having friendly exchanges and seemed to be getting along quite well.

Before I knew it, summer had arrived, and there were new opportunities to make money. My friend Henry and I partnered up and sold fireworks with a number of other people in the office building. It would be a ten-day windfall for both of us. We rented a nice space next to Shopko, a discount store similar to Kmart. We worked feverishly building our fireworks stand. All the product would be fronted to us, and we would pay when we were done.

We opened ten days before the Fourth of July. We seemed to have our stuff together much better than anyone else. As we stocked the shelves, we realized that something was not quite right. Sure we had bottle rockets, roman candles, multi-shot cannons, and a few other powerful items, but no firecrackers, none of the smaller items. Our selection was far from complete.

We were only open a couple of hours before the fire marshal arrived. He explained that half of the products we had on display were illegal to sell in our county. Our great big beautiful dream had just fallen in the toilet. It was worse than horrible. It was the end of the line for me.

Henry stayed calm and clear. He approached our competitor and explained that we needed to buy fireworks at wholesale. To my amazement, they set up an account for us and sold us anything and everything we needed. Over the next ten days, we cleared almost $900 each. Not a bad income and a disaster avoided in my life.

It was time to prepare for the fair in August. I was feeling good about myself and my life. Again I was talking every day to Jane. I could always find an excuse. I felt successful and friendly. I turned on the charm, and bingo, she let down her defenses. Life couldn't be any better.

Marian called. She was in town and needed a place to stay. I said, "Sure, you can stay with me." I was so excited. I wanted to open my home to her.

It wasn't fifteen minutes after Marian arrived that Jane was knocking at the door. Marian had walked into the bedroom to hang her clothes. I opened the door, and Jane burst in saying, "Who's here?" She walked into the living room demanding, "I want to know who's here now."

I stuttered, "It's Marian. She's just visiting."

"What is SHE doing here?" Jane's voice was raised.

"Nothing," I said. "She just needed a place to stay."

"SO, you're sleeping with her!"

"No, I don't want anything to do with her," I said. I was freaked out. I wanted to tell the truth, but the lies flew out of my mouth.

"I don't have to take this kind of treatment," she said. "I'm out of here." As she left, she slammed the door behind her.

Marian walked out of the bedroom. Talk about two worlds colliding! She had overheard my conversation with Jane. "I'm out of here," she said. "You haven't changed."

"Okay, sorry," was all I could muster.

"I just can't believe it!" she said. "I don't have to put up with that kind of shit." She gathered her things and was gone.

I sat down on the couch and started to cry. What was going on? I knew that God must hate me. How could I have such bad luck? Some power greater than me had caught me again doing something I was not supposed to do. Except this time I was caught for doing something that was only wrong in Jane's mind, not mine. I knew it was not my fault. It was just me being screwed again by life. I smoked a joint and laid my head on the couch and went to sleep.

I awoke to someone knocking on the front door. It was Jane with Jennifer in her arms. "I want to talk to you."

I stepped back from the door. "Sure, come on in." I walked back to the couch and sat on one end. Jane sat on the far end and set Jennifer down between us.

"What was that bleached blond cunt doing here?" she asked. She was angry but not loud. I panicked and was suddenly filled with fear. I couldn't speak without lying. I couldn't think.

"She just stopped by," I said. "I didn't know she was coming."

"Did you sleep with her last night?"

"No. No I did not."

Her voice was rising. "How long have you been seeing her behind my back?"

I could barely hear what Jane was saying. I was numb. I remembered a time when my father wanted to talk about something I had done wrong. The anxiety was more than I could handle, and I had literally blanked out. The same thing was happening to me here. Defenses were up and in place without having to think. It was automatic and very powerful. I didn't care what the truth was. I knew I was in trouble, and getting out of trouble was the only thing I cared about.

Jane stood up, screaming, "You bastard! You have been fucking that blond cunt haven't you?" She swung at me with a closed fist and missed. I grabbed Jennifer from the couch. I knew I now had the upper hand. She was completely out of control. I was in control. And I knew I was in trouble.

"You have to leave," I said. With baby in hand, I grabbed Jane by the arm and escorted her to the door.

She was screaming, "Give me my baby, you bastard!"

I kept her moving and said, "I'll give her to you when you settle down." As we passed through the doorway, Jane took another swing at me and connected with the door jam.

She walked quickly to her truck, saying, "Look what you did." She opened the door and climbed in. I handed Jennifer to her, and she strapped her into the car seat. She started the truck, then turned to me and said, "You asshole. You are going to pay for this."

As the truck backed up with tires spinning, I picked up a handful of gravel and threw it at the windshield, breaking it. She stopped the truck, and I retreated into the house. She got out, picked up a brick from the planter, and threw it through my front window. "You are going to jail, you bastard," she yelled. Both my window and her windshield were broken.

After she left, I panicked. I knew I was in serious trouble. I could hardly sleep all night. I could smoke a lot of pot, but no matter how stoned I got, my mind continued to search for a way out. My previous conviction for domestic abuse hung over my head. How was I going to keep from going to jail? I knew I would have to serve six months if I were convicted again. There was no doubt in my mind I was going to jail for six months. I had finally gone too far. Again, screwed by life.

I awoke early the next morning. I could not believe what I could remember about the night before. I tried calling Jane, with no luck. It was clearly time for damage control. I knew she had an appointment with her lawyer at noon.

I ordered Jane a single sterling rose. I wrote her a letter expressing my deep and sincere apologies for my behavior. I was completely guilty and would do anything, anything it took to get my butt out of this terrible jam.

I went to the city attorney, willing to throw myself on the mercy of anyone who would listen. Nobody was buying. I was screwed, and it wasn't my fault. Or maybe it was. But who cares now, I just knew I had to get out of this trouble.

I called my friend Robin in Louisiana. I would leave town, anything to keep out of jail. I could not deal with the idea of going to jail. I would agree to anything.

As luck, or a great manipulator, would have it, I was able to make a deal. If I would give up all my furniture, promise to pay five thousand dollars, give up my custody rights, promise to stay away from Jane, and only see my daughter when Jane wanted me to, I would receive a reprieve. All visits would be handled through a mediator. Against the advice of my attorney, I agreed. No one could understand the power that going to jail for the next six months had over me.

How did I get here? The last time I walked out of jail, I had promised myself never again, no matter what. Yet here I was, teetering on the edge of serving six months. I had to change something so I would never get this close again.

A new plan. I joined a therapy group for men who had been court-ordered to attend a program for ending violence in relationships. It was easy, but just like everything else, I didn't let my guard down. It was in these meetings that I met Dr. Sandra. She assisted in facilitating the meetings and specialized in abused children. From the moment I met her, I felt something special existed between us.

Every week I attended the meeting, and went home knowing that nothing was really going to change. I was going through the motions but was not changing. I was depressed but not aware of it. Hopelessness surrounded me. I thought about dying constantly. I finally gave in to the idea that death was an acceptable way to end my suffering. All hope was removed from me. Nothing was working. Then one evening Dr. Sandra announced her decision to practice at the local mental health center. I asked if she would see me privately at the center, and she agreed.

I am sure she was surprised at how quickly I made my first appointment. I had to do something to get the evil out of me. If I could not control it, I did not want my life. I had to do something more to insure I would never get myself in this much trouble again.

My mind went on overtime, turning over and over all the possibilities. What was the root of the problem? It had to be somewhere outside of me, because I sure as hell knew it was not being caused by me. The idea persisted that maybe it was coming from something that had happened to me in childhood. Perhaps the answer to "why am I always screwed out of everything I really want?" was in my childhood.

I hauled a small homemade wooden typing table and an old IBM Selectric typewriter in from the garage. I started a blank page and placed the numbers 1953, then a space, then 1954, and so on down the page until I reached 1989. Then, as I would think about an event in my past, I would write a note under the year it happened. Holidays, birthdays, family trips, anything and everything that came up, I would enter it where it belonged.

I started with my earliest memories, organizing all the events of my past. As each memory came up, I wrote down the year and event. Christmases were easy, then the Fourth of Julys, then Easters and Thanksgivings. The remembering of each event seemed to lead me to more memories and events. They just kept coming out.

I sat and wrote for twenty minutes, then a flood of memories overwhelmed me. My body reacted with unbelievable physical pain. Within twenty minutes, I found myself unable to endure the pain, and I retreated to lay on bed.

My mind was reeling from the overload. I had never felt such pain. I could not numb myself to it. It consumed my entire being. I kept telling myself, "This is it. This will change my life."

Minutes turned into hours, hours into days, and days into weeks. Every day, I spent the entire day writing and feeling. I would write until a memory came clear to me. Then my body would respond with pain. It usually started in my butt and then would move down my thighs, legs, and ankles. It was very real and would totally paralyze me. It was like when I was a kid and my dad was whipping me. It was sharp and overwhelming. It felt unstoppable, like it would never end. I could only lay and feel the pain.

There was no time for sleep, just the time of laying and waiting for my body to recover. Once a week, I went to private therapy and to group therapy. That was my entire life. Cigarettes, water, and a little food were all I needed to explore the territory of my childhood. It was slow to start with, but every day it grew. The phone did not ring, and nobody stopped to visit. The lack of interruptions allowed me to stay present, but it was sheer determination that carried me through the darkest moments. I was not going to live this way any longer. I was going to change my world or die.

After two months of continuous writing, my weight was down fifty pounds, the confessional was complete, and there would be no going back.

It was time to pay bills and be a responsible person again. I was surprised that my finances were not in worse shape. Sure I was broke, but my attitude was in a place of being able to start over.

Surprisingly, when I finished the book, I was also through with Jane. In the past, each time I had quit my addiction to her, I knew I would never go back. And each time, I had ended up proving to myself that I was lying. The restraining order had forced me to back off from her, but it was not my choice. Writing the book was the final time for me to have any thoughts of getting back together with her. Finishing it was me choosing what I wanted. I made the choice to heal from the hell I had created for myself with Jane. I had tried to break away from her so many times before. The thing that made this time different was I made it.

Milestones

As I stepped back into life, I had one world, the world of Lee. The world of Jane was gone forever. It was time to commit myself to the world of Lee and make it work.

Being intentional with my relationships with women over the past 18 months had shown me that I could be myself and develop friendships with women without losing control.

I was no longer an abused animal lashing out at those who mistreated me. I could take responsibility for my response to others and to life. Having discharged the feelings and memories from childhood, I now saw myself as healed, rather than injured. Life was no longer overwhelming.

I began to get the answer to why I was always screwed out of everything I wanted. It wasn't a curse. It was my inability or unwillingness to take responsibility for my own life.

One night, I met my neighbor, Lynn. She gave me a brief opportunity to develop a relationship with her and yet hold onto myself. She was a redhead, and her energy was wild and exciting. Her boyfriend had gone to South Dakota to participate in an experiment testing products on humans, and he would not be home for several months.

We talked and walked every few days. Her son Damian hung out with me and enjoyed reading the story of my childhood. I was back working at the office building and making deals. My life was finally on the right track.

I could be with Lynn and not feel out of control or threatened. There was nothing to come of the relationship, just friendship. Knowing that, I didn't put expectations on the future. I was able to just be with her, enjoying every minute, knowing it could be the last. We both enjoyed smoking a little pot, drinking a little wine, eating exquisite food, and sharing our bodies with each other. I felt valuable, liked, and honest.

I lost interest in seeing Jane. When Lynn had time for me, great. When she didn't, that was fine too. I had plenty to do. Life was very good. On the morning of my birthday, there was a knock at the front door. It was the little redhead, and she had a plan, some pot, a bottle of Cold Duck, and very few clothes. By the end of the day, I had promised myself that I would never undervalue my birthday again.

It was only a few days before Christmas when Lynn's boyfriend returned home. I had already purchased presents for her and Damian. I knew that he was expected, I just didn't expect it to happen so fast.

Lynn was an angel who came breathing life into a soul who was dying. I can't really explain, but I didn't feel bad that her boyfriend had returned. I was so grateful for the new lease on life I was experiencing, I didn't have time to regret that she would no longer be a part of my life, at least not in the way she had been for the past three months.

A court hearing on the custody was set for late January. I had fired my last attorney and hired a new one to help me. I arrived in court expecting it to be just a formality. The judge started asking questions, and I stammered and stuttered, "I work for myself; uh. I don't make very much; uh. I pay what I can."

It was a short hearing. I would be allowed to see Jennifer every other weekend and once during the week. Jennifer would be dropped in front of a minister's house, and I was to be in back. There would be no direct contact between Jane and me. The judge told me I had better find a real job, if I wanted to have any future with this little girl.

I was in a small recovery group with a man named Jim, who owned a full-service outdoor sign company. On Thursday night, I asked Jim if he could use a good employee. He said he could. I suggested I ride with him for a couple of days, and we would decide if I could work in his company. On the very first day, I liked his style. He was laid back and totally comfortable with his life. Jim didn't talk much and always made light of things.

By the second day, I had decided I would enjoy working for him. I could see how I would be an asset. He invited Sheila, his partner and wife, to have lunch with us. At our first meeting, I had the strangest feeling that she and I had met before. She was petite, blue-eyed, and blond.

It was clear that Jim and Sheila were not getting along. The energy around them was very tense. We agreed I would work for them. The starting pay was far below what I thought I was worth, but it would do to start. I knew that given a little time they would see my value, and I could earn much more. Besides, the judge had said a "RJ," Real Job. I shuddered at the thought.

Things with Jane were rough. For my visits with Jennifer, Jane showed up when she wanted to and sometimes not at all. Sometimes she had a boyfriend with her and made a scene. One time the police came and arrested me for violating my restraining order. I posted bond and didn't even go to jail. The next day the judge dropped the charges. No evidence.

I was still under the restraining order and was not allowed to contact Jane other than through my attorney. There was going to be another hearing, and I had to document everything she was doing and turn it over to the judge. I was sure she was trying to destroy me.

One day she stopped coming completely. The next visit there was still no Jane or Jennifer, and the next, and the next. This continued for a couple of months. The divorce was finished except for the issue of visitation and custody. It was a living nightmare, with my attorney writing her attorney until a court date was finally set. Jane would have to appear and explain why she was not letting me see Jennifer.

Jim gave me lots of room to explore and learn his business, and Sheila really seemed to appreciate the breath of fresh air I brought. She was supportive and encouraged my ideas for improving their company. They both seemed to care deeply about other people and their problems.

I worked hard and loved being a part of their business. As the days passed, I learned more about the intimate workings of the company. Jim and Sheila were separated and considering divorce. Jim had a girlfriend, and Sheila was dating, too. Their recent history had been rough, with lots of infidelity, disagreements, and distrust.

I had only been there a few weeks when I realized there was something going on between Sheila and me, and I wanted to take it further. Jim was sitting alone in his small office in the main shop when I walked in. I sat down beside him and posed the question, "Jim, how would you feel about me asking Sheila out?"

He turned and smiled. "You would be doing me a great favor. Maybe it will give her something to focus on besides me." I was surprised and appreciative.

I was infatuated with this interesting woman. She was cute, wounded, and fun to be around. I could not wait to invite her to do something with me. I was still committed to the idea of no sex, just friendship with women. I was enjoying the companionship of other women in this way, and it was very safe. For Sheila, I had the same thoughts. Hell, I worked for her. We could be great friends, but nothing more. It was another opportunity for me to experiment with being in a relationship with a woman and not having sex.

I invited Sheila to go for a hike one evening. I didn't consider it a date, just a couple of friends going for a little hike. I considered going to dinner or a movie to be a date, but a short evening hike, that was innocent. I could hardly believe how easy she was to be around. She had a soft, gentle smile, and her eyes lit up a room. I could see a beautiful young girl hiding inside her. I called her Sheila. Sheila was my boss, and Sheila was the beautiful girl I saw inside her.

At work, I advanced from digging holes for foundations to driving a service truck and making sales. I went to my group ACOD meetings every Friday night and continued to see Dr. Sandra once a week. She was especially instrumental in my survival by being an advocate for the part of me that had been abused by everyone. My life was full now of nurturing and caring people.

The legal battle continued with Jane. I'd still had no contact with Jennifer, and my attorney had set up another hearing with the judge. It was to be a private meeting in his chambers. Jane was going through attorneys like crazy. She was on attorney number six at this time.

When my attorney and I arrived at the judge's chambers, we were escorted in. It was a conference room with the judge sitting at the head of the table, Jane on one side, and my attorney and me on the other. It was clear that Jane was alone. The judge asked where her attorney was, and she explained that her most recent attorney had been dismissed.

My attorney addressed the judge and explained that I had not seen my daughter in several months, that I had a job, and that there was no reason for me being kept apart from my daughter. The judge asked Jane why she had not been abiding by the temporary visitation agreement. Jane replied she had evidence that Jennifer had been molested by me.

I could not believe my ears. This was crazy! The judge said that until further order I would only be allowed to see Jennifer in a supervised visitation. He then ordered that an attorney be appointed Guardian Ad Litem for Jennifer. She would investigate the situation and report back to the judge.

My head felt like it was exploding. I was afraid I would throw up. I could not believe that all it took was an accusation for me to be screwed again. My new attorney was absolutely worthless. It was all I could do to maintain control and not explode.

Twice a week I was allowed a one-hour visit with Jennifer. I was not allowed to be alone with her. The visits were at the Watson's Children's Home, where I had been doing volunteer work for the past year. Sheila had painted and donated a sign to them. I felt understood and accepted by all the employees and the owner, Janis Watson. She operated the home from a wheelchair and was always loving, supportive, and compassionate toward me.

It was required that someone from the Children's Home sit in the room with me while I played with my daughter. This was fine for a couple of weeks until Jane did the old no-show trick again. It was predictable, at least for me. She had missed two visits and then I received a letter. Jane had moved. She was now living in Stanford, a very small farming community about 250 miles away.

For the next three months my attorney wrote letters to her new attorney in Stanford. Carol, the guardian appointed to watch out for Jennifer's interest, was unsure how to proceed. I had tried everything I could think of and was at the end of my rope.

I made an appointment with Carol and arrived at her office with the clear intent of ending this war. I sat down and said, "I've had enough. Everything that's going on is clearly not in the best interest of my daughter. "

"I'm through," I said. "I won't fight any more."

Carol looked me square in the eye and asked, "Do you love your daughter?"

My response was instantaneous. "Yes," I said, "and that's why I'm ending this."

She wrote a few words on the back of one of her business cards and pushed it across the desk. It had the name "Kerry Mitchell" and a "$." She said, "He's expensive and worth it. Go see him."

I scratched my head on the way down the stairs. I didn't want to keep up the fight, but... what if I could win? Carol pushing that card across the desk was clearly a sign to continue to fight for my rights and my daughter's rights. As I passed through the downstairs doors, I saw it was a beautiful day.

I got an appointment for early the next week with Kerry. At our first meeting, I knew this attorney was different than any I had ever met. He was very professional and direct. He reviewed my case files and said, "This will be expensive and will take a long time to straighten out." I nodded, but I could not see how it would be possible to straighten out this mess. "I will need a retainer of $1,500. I will also need a guarantor and an agreement to meet the requirements regarding payment of my bills." All I could do was sit and agree.

I arrived back at Sheila's office and explained the situation. I told her that I needed $1,500 in cash for the retainer to hire this new attorney. I explained what had happened in the attorney's office. She suggested that she and Jim might be willing to help me.

The next day Sheila told me they would loan me the money and deduct a little from my paycheck each week until it was paid back. She also agreed to personally co-sign for the balance of the fees. I couldn't believe the generosity being offered. This was a new beginning for me.

I had always gotten people to help me in the past, and eventually they would give up or leave. I had a long trail of unfinished or incomplete relationships and agreements. Now, a virtual stranger believed in me enough to loan me money and risk an unknown future. I could not conceive the magnitude this act of kindness would have on my future, but I understood that this time, I would have to get it right.

Starting that day I could walk a little taller. I knew someone saw something in me worth believing in. That knowledge was enough to light up my life.

The new attorney, Kerry, was a whole new level of representation. He knew how to get what he wanted. Over the next year, I learned that as crazy as Jane was, there was someone who knew how to deal with her kind. Having Kerry representing me was almost as powerful as having Sheila believe in me.

I continued to work for Jim and Sheila through the summer. I was having the time of my life. I was in control, and everything was going my way. I had finally figured out the solution to my life.

Sheila and I were seeing each other every moment we could find. We were very discrete, but I am sure it was obvious to the other employees that something was going on between us.

I still lived in my little apartment in Harvest Creek. It was set back off the road, surrounded by trees and very quiet. Sheila had her family home. Her daughter, Kay, was still in high school and living at home.

Then Jim began to quietly sabotage jobs that I was working on. He came in one weekend and worked on a project I had sold, "accidentally" drilling holes in the wrong places. It ruined the project and created delays which made me look bad. He did it "innocently," but I knew better. I have a very keen sense of when people are hiding their true feelings, so I approached him and asked what was going on. He shared that he believed we needed to find a different way to relate. With all the stuff going on between him, Sheila, and me, he suggested I find another job. I was not surprised. I could see he really cared for Sheila and was hurt by the two of us playing together.

I agreed that I should leave. The nine months of working with him had been healing and beneficial, but I was ready to move on.

I was now driving two hundred fifty miles to Stanford, Montana every other weekend to visit with Jennifer. Sheila was always with me. The judge had dismissed all notions that there was anything inappropriate going on between my daughter and me. He ordered that I have full visitation. For my protection, Sheila volunteered to accompany me on my visits. She was willing to do anything to help me and gave freely of her time and energy.

We drove every other weekend to see Jennifer. We picked her up in the small town of Stanford, population 146. It was just a spot in the road. We took her back to Great Falls and spent the night in a hotel, swimming, eating, and enjoying being together.

I left the sign company and approached one of my customers, Martin, who owned a hotel, bar, and restaurant. The restaurant was closed. I asked him if he would lease it to me on a percentage basis. I then approached my friends Bonnie and Henry to be investors in my project. They agreed to loan me $2,000, and away I went on a new adventure.

A chef who had worked for the previous owner was living in the hotel and offered to partner with me. I accepted his offer. The future was filled with green lights and magic.

I knew little about the restaurant business, but lack of knowledge had never slowed me down before. When I looked at new ventures, I tended to see them as perfect, not seeing any of the flaws. Sheila, on the other hand, tended to see all the problems with anything we looked at. So when it came to the restaurant, I only showed her what I wanted her to see because I didn't want her to stop liking me.

It was only a few weeks before Sheila announced that she was going to finalize her divorce and leave the sign company, too. She was going to rent out the family home, take a job with an excavating company, and move in with me. Wow-my life had just moved into warp speed.

Soon there was another hearing, with the judge listening to me, Dr. Sandra, Jennifer's guardian, and Jane. Dr. Sandra and the judge held a conversation with each other in front of all of us.

The judge asked what she suggested he do. She explained that Jane was the only one feeling threatened by me and that I posed no danger to Jennifer. The judge ordered joint custody and plenty of visitation for me, meaning every other weekend and a month during the summer. This was a milestone in the strengthening of my confidence and self esteem. I had given up trying to win against Jane, and now I was being rewarded with the knowledge that there were people in the world who believed in me and would stand up for me.

It was October of 1992, and Jennifer was four years old. Sheila was living with me and working for the excavation company. I was still at work in the restaurant. Suddenly the hotel was crawling with men in suits. This was Bozeman, Montana. A suit was not normal attire for anyone other than lawyers and undertakers. These men appeared to be from the city. They were definitely not local.

A short, heavyset man entered the restaurant and approached the hostess. He explained that nobody was to touch anything. They would be counting the money and taking an inventory. I shot out of the kitchen and told this man in the suit that I owned the restaurant. He explained that I owned nothing, that the hotel had been placed in receivership, and that all leases were canceled. Any complaints could be directed to the District Court. I explained that there was a lot going on and I needed to know what to do. He said they would work with me. I would just have to be patient.

It was devastating. I did stick around and eventually spoke with them. I explained that my Christmas bonus was based on the Christmas parties. They agreed to employ me for 30 days to help with the parties. I worked the parties and was laid off right before Christmas. I earned a little money but no Christmas bonus. At least I had the satisfaction of not abandoning my customers.

Life was not over. We had been planning a trip to Las Vegas, and I now felt good enough about myself to believe I could survive Christmas with my family. Except for the day I'd introduced Jane to my mom, I had not seen my family for fifteen years. Everyone would be at my mom's for the holiday. My sister Jenny and her husband Tommy were driving from Texas, and Al and his girlfriend lived in Vegas. Eddie and his wife also lived in Vegas, and my baby sister Dee would be home from college. Even the old man would be there.

It was just a few days before Christmas. I reserved a new Dodge van from Dollar Rental. It would be the perfect 10 days, just Sheila, Jennifer, and me.

We arrived in the early evening and went directly to our motel room. We were staying in an Econolodge near downtown. Jenny and Tommy had reservations at the same motel.

My mom lived on the edge of North Las Vegas in an old trailer court. There was an old bar and used car lot between Mom's trailer and the boulevard.

After unpacking at the motel, we headed to Mom's. I was excited and felt safe. Father had divorced Mom, and he seldom came to her house. I knew he would have no power at her place.

We arrived at the trailer before dark. Everyone greeted each other with hugs and handshakes. I had my video camera and so did Tommy and Eddie. It was amazing. All my brothers and sisters were together for Christmas.

We spent a total of four days with my family. The second day was Christmas Eve, and everyone gathered at Mom's. Even the old man showed up. When he and I were in the same room, he became extremely quiet. Sheila told me that when I left the room, he would light up and become the life of the party. As soon as I returned, he became quiet. I too could feel the discomfort but was very in control of my feelings. The evening ended quietly.

We headed back to Mom's on Christmas Day. We arrived early and shared breakfast and the opening of presents. I joined Al, Jenny, Tommy, and their kids in a little driveway football.

Evening came, and we traveled to Eddie's house. He had a mansion on the hill overlooking Las Vegas. Jennifer commented that Uncle Eddie must live in a hotel. It was a large two-story house set on an acre of ground. There were electric gates at the entrance. We drove in to face the largest garage I have ever seen. It held at least six cars with plenty of room left over.

We entered through the garage. The first room in the house was large with cathedral ceilings. It was breathtaking. Upstairs on one end were bedrooms and the maid's quarters. Downstairs was a kitchen and more bedrooms. On the other end were stairs leading up to a huge family room over the garage. There was a full-service bar, pool table, exercise equipment, computer area, and television area. There were large sliding-glass doors that led to a balcony overlooking the city. It was very impressive.

Father lived in a small cottage on the far side of the property. He had been living with Eddie and his family for several years. I did not understand their relationship. To hear Eddie talk, he was a hero taking care of the old man. To listen to Father, Eddie owed him from some deal or another that had gone bad in the past. It was clear they didn't speak to each other about it.

The evening was fabulous, with cocktails, snacks, and conversation. Father joined the party for a short visit. I sensed his discomfort when I greeted him and chose to keep my distance the remainder of the evening.

I was jealous of Eddie and all he had. I questioned whether the choices I had made in my life were the correct ones. I didn't think about it too much. I looked around and recognized that I could never find happiness in any of what he had, and I quickly assured myself that this was not the success I was looking for.

One more day with the family and then we would be off to California. Morning came quickly. Mom suggested we take the children to a recreation center in a mall. Jennifer loved playing with her cousins. Sheila, my mom, Dee, and myself were left to entertain ourselves in the adult area.

The conversation was the regular empty chitchat. All of a sudden I heard talk of "being family" and a future of being family. I exploded with, "What family?" I tried to control myself, but the words shot out of my mouth. I looked at my mom. "Let's get one thing clear," I said. "I will never call you Mom."

"You can be Jennifer's grandma. I have good memories of Grandma. But I will never call you Mom. If you are willing to start a relationship with me having that ground rule, then I am open to getting to know you."

Everyone was quiet. Then Mom answered, "Yes, you can call me Grandma."

That was not enough for me. I wanted more. The words spewed forth. "You were a terrible mom. You should have protected us. I really hate you for what you did not do. I need to know that you understand how mad I am at you."

Mom was calm and collected. She responded, "It's fine if you want to call me Grandma."

What a relief. I started breathing again. I could not understand how she could listen to my anger and not reject me. Instead, she was willing to accept my terms for a relationship. At that moment I knew something special had happened. I could feel it in my bones, all the way to my soul.

The next morning, we departed. The trip to Las Vegas had moved something inside me. In my heart something was different. A new possibility existed. I had no idea what lay ahead, and I did not care. I had made it across a huge obstacle in my life.

The next three months were heaven on earth. I was not working. Sheila sold her house, and we spent time skiing and rebuilding a wrecked car for Kay. Everything was simple and quiet.

Spring arrived bringing with it new possibilities. Early one morning the phone rang, and it was Martin. He had recovered the hotel. "Are you interested in being General Manager of the whole property?" he asked.

Without hesitation, I said, "Yes." It was a dream come true. I can still remember Dr. Sandra's question. She asked, "What is your image of a hotel manager?"

I replied, "None."

"Good," she said. "Now be the type of manager that fits you. You will never be disappointed."

Everything in life was a crisis for me. I was always on the defensive, always planning for the moment when the other shoe would drop. On the outside I looked calm, but the exact opposite was true. I worried all the time. I believed if I worried enough I would have control of what was happening to me and around me. I lived in constant stress trying to control the world. I believed I had the power to control my environment.

The next morning Martin and I met at the hotel to take possession. I believed I had finally made it. I was on top of the world, yet the need to live on guard was as strong as it had ever been. I was a good manager. It was perfect for me. I was the perfect mix between a maintenance man and a real hotel manager. I worked hard and controlled everything and everyone in my presence. Martin did not know how long he would be able to hold on to the hotel, but he trusted me to help him recover as much of his previous losses as possible.

As fall approached, Jennifer was about to start kindergarten. Jane and I had always agreed that Valley Christian School in Bozeman was the best school anywhere for Jennifer. We were interviewed by board members of the school, and Jennifer was accepted as a student. Jane moved to Bozeman. It was a miracle for me. I had dreamed of attending Jennifer's school and being involved with her life. This was another milestone in my healing. I believed God had forgiven me.

Quitting smoking was another milestone in my journey to healing. I had spent my entire life without ever being in touch with my body, my feelings, or my thoughts. I constantly used something to alter my natural state of being, whether it was drugs, alcohol, food, cigarettes, television, sex, talking, relationships, or work. I knew that quitting smoking cigarettes would change my life and force me to be present to my feelings, my body, and my life.

After three weeks of not smoking, Sheila and everyone I worked with had had enough. I arrived home one evening to my apartment, and Sheila said, "You're being a jerk to everyone, and I've had it. You can start being nice or move to the hotel." I chose being nice. For the next three months I really missed smoking, but then life started getting better and better.

Jennifer had become a little person. She had a mind and an opinion and was not afraid to say what she wanted. Being around her was another big milestone in my healing. I found myself watching her every move, thought, and action. I was in total wonder about this little person. I thought, "This is what I would have been like if my parents had loved me."

Since moving back to Bozeman, nothing was easy for Jane. A decent job eluded her. She struggled to pay her bills and fell deeper in debt every month. She continued to work part time and worked at Jennifer's school to help with her tuition.

Life for me, on the other hand, had never been so good. Sheila and I had agreed that my little apartment was too confining for the two of us. She moved to her own place, and I had my apartment back to myself. Our relationship continued to grow in leaps and bounds. We still did most things together, but the space offered a freshness that we both appreciated.

Christmas arrived, and I was on top of my game with Jennifer in town. Her being in a Christian school placed a lot of focus on family, Christ, and the whole Christmas trip. All the people at Jennifer's school were very nice, but I kept my guard up. If I were confronted regarding the Christian belief system, I would be in serious trouble. I constantly rehearsed my responses to imaginary questions. I was always careful not to express my thoughts one way or the other. I was afraid of being found out to be an imposter. I was there for Jennifer and what was best for her. This was another milestone in my journey, experiencing that there were things in the world that were more important to me than "me."

As the new year rolled around, Martin lost the hotel again. It seemed that my life had just gotten great and another disaster came blasting in. It was also time for the AA Agape, an annual weekend that brought people together to share, care, and carry the message of service, unity, and fellowship. I had been attending them for the past couple of years and found that spending a weekend with people practicing unconditional love and acceptance always nurtured my soul. This one was no different. I arrived to find familiar faces and friends ready to spend a weekend without judgments.

It was on Sunday afternoon that I found an article in a magazine called Miracles. It spoke of a Quadrinity Process to integrate the four fundamental dimensions of our being, the intellect, emotions, body, and spirit. I read it intensely and knew it was the answer to my prayers. It was an 8-day residential intensive workshop that spoke of resolving seemingly immovable blocks to self-awareness, happiness, loving relationships, spirituality, career, family life, and freedom from addictions. Oh my God!

Monday could not come fast enough for me. I called the Hoffman Institute and discovered the next workshop was only a month away. Perfect. I would borrow a friend's pickup and drive myself down and back. I was going to California and would return a new person.

March was a beautiful time of year. The drive from Montana to Northern California would take a couple of days, and I would travel through Carson, the town I had run away from almost twenty years ago.

I left early and drove all day, stopping only for gas and treats. I spent the first night in a small motel in Winnemucca. As I got closer to Carson, I felt a sense of fear and loss. I could remember all the times I had driven that same road.

Memories flooded over me. I was carrying a tape recorder and documented the entire trip. I talked into the recorder to share with Sheila the experience I was having. I recorded my feelings, thoughts, and ideas. Someday she would hear this and share my soul-transforming adventure.

To my surprise, good memories were mixed with the bad ones, and the good outnumbered the bad. As I drove through Carson, everything seemed familiar but more like a movie I had once seen. I was hoping to touch base with a couple of my old friends, but nothing panned out. There was a strong feeling of peace and calm filling me from the inside. I was not as bad as I had remembered.

I graduated from the Hoffman Institute a changed person. I was free for the second time in my life. Everything made sense to me, religion, people, the planet, relationships. I felt deeply and completely connected to everything, a cellular-level experience. The last thing they said as we left was, "Your homework is to unconditionally love and accept your parents." The words bounced off the excitement of being fixed. There had never been a time in my life that I felt so in touch with God, the universe, and myself. Magic was alive and well inside me. I had power over my world.

I took two full days to drive home. It was part of the process to spend two days adjusting to all that had happened in the last eight. I left at 3:00 am to give me time to adjust to the new wonder I was experiencing. My senses were extremely heightened. I was raw. I was fully functioning. The world was brighter, louder, and moving faster than I was ready for. My mind raced freely, examining all the sights, sounds, and information I was taking in. I felt so gentle, so open and loving. All the strangers I met were receptive and open to my presence. I had what I wanted plus more than I had imagined possible.

Arriving in Bozeman, I stopped at Sheila's first. I wanted her to see the new me, the caring me, the unplugged me, the me who was at peace with the world. She recognized the difference right away. I was in a state of wonder and amazement. Being gone always made coming home wonderful, but somehow this was different. It was magical and unique. I was closer to Sheila now than I had ever known being close to anyone.

I returned to my apartment and knew that everything would be different from now on.

I had left my little pickup with my friend Willy to try and sell while I was gone. I returned to find he had not been able to get it sold, but with my new outlook on life, everything was beautiful. Nothing could disturb my peace of mind. For the next two weeks I advertised the little truck for sale and explored other opportunities to earn a little money.

Finally, a guy named Dave came along and offered me $3,800. I was asking $4,400 and felt it was a fair price. Now I started to question myself. I took Dave's number and told him I would consider his offer. Over the next couple of days, I wrestled with whether to take the cash in hand or hold out for what I thought the truck was worth. I went crazy trying to make this decision. The arguing in my head was out of control. I hated to take $600 less than it was worth, but I had bills that were overdue. I called Dave and told him I would take his offer. He asked me to bring the truck to his home the next day.

I arrived right on time, title in hand, and satisfied I had made a good choice. Dave invited me in. It was a fancy apartment. He counted out $3,300 on the counter then said he had come up a little short. I was dumbfounded. I pushed to get one word out. "What?" I could not even think.

He said, "I'm a gem dealer and would be happy to give you the balance in precious stones. I'll give them to you wholesale, and you can make a few bucks yourself."

I stuttered, "Well, I guess I can look at what you have." I had gone totally numb from head to toe. I could not leave here now without everything I could get. I believed now that nobody was going to buy my truck and I was too far behind on my bills not to take whatever deal he offered.

He laid out boxes of stones. I knew nothing about gems but did the best I could to pick out ones I thought would be valuable to sell. I pretended I was cool with everything. I was such a nice guy. Dave gave me a ride home.

As I walked into my apartment, I knew something big had just happened. I was too numb to know what it was. I had already forgotten my sense of peace and trust in the universe. I had gone back to trusting only what was in my hand. I thought taking a "bad" deal was the best I could hope to do. I sat down and started paying my bills. Oh, what a good feeling it was to pay my bills. Everything was all right now.

Over the next couple of days, the numbness began to wear off. I expected to return to the euphoria I had experienced the past couple of weeks, but it was gone. I was back where I had started before I went to the Institute. I had heard of other people losing what they had found. They had been able to get it back, and so could I. Every day I practiced the exercises and listened to the tapes. Within a week, I was dedicating hours a day to getting back to Nirvana. I dedicated more and more time, but nothing worked. I had lost it.

I took a part time job selling business listings for RL Polk's directory. I made decent money, but my heart wasn't in it. I found that I was willing to cheat to win. I was angry about life and about having to do this crappy job.

By fall, I agreed to share my apartment with an acquaintance, John, from my men's group. I was so shut down that the only feelings to escape were those that popped out when I was not looking. I had to protect myself at any cost.

Right after the holidays, Jane announced she was joining her boyfriend in Sun Valley. She knew she could get work there, and she really hated living in Bozeman. I agreed to have Jennifer live with me to finish the school year. I purchased a bunk bed and set it up in the smaller room. Jennifer and I would share a bedroom. We lay in our beds and talked every night before going to sleep. I was her fulltime caregiver. I was in heaven. Jane was gone, and for the first time since Jennifer's birth, I felt the full impact of being a father. This was something that I had never believed was going to happen, and now it was reality.

I had to find work now, and it had to allow for Jennifer being in my life. I was finally willing to give up the idea of "getting rich quick." I had something more important than getting rich. I had spent most of the energy in my life "working at getting out of working." Chasing rainbows. Now I had a daughter who needed and depended on me. What had been important all my life had just changed.

One morning I woke up with the idea that I should go to work selling for an electric sign company. There were only two in town, Jim's and another company that had been around forever and had gotten lazy. I knew Jer who worked for a sign company in Helena, 100 miles away. He had been there for years, and I knew he would give me the inside track and help me get on with them.

I called, and they were not hiring salesmen. I explained that I offered something very different from the "normal" salesman. For the next month, I talked with them on the phone and convinced them that they really needed to at least look at what I had to offer. I was so sure that this was the job for me that I didn't even apply at other places. During the interview, I was so confident I would be hired that I wasn't afraid to share my honest self in a pleasing way.

Of course, I was hired. I was able to get Jennifer off to school and start work by 9:00. I quit by 2:30 each day to pick Jennifer up after school. It was truly a dream come true for me. It did not take long before I had commissions starting to flow. I had virtually no debt, except the old bills left from years ago, and so the money I earned was plenty for the two of us.

Four months of being totally responsible for Jennifer's care ignited a new fire in me. I wanted to earn a living, be responsible, and have Jennifer in my life.

Summer arrived all too soon. The week before school was out, Jennifer said, "My mom is picking me up after school on Thursday, and we're going to Idaho." I called and called Jane's number but only got an answering machine. I left several messages asking Jane to call me. I was upset that Jane was taking Jennifer out of school a day early. I dialed Jane's number at least 25 times within two days.

Finally, she answered the phone, and I told her, "Jennifer has school on Friday, and she wants to attend the last day of school." Jane's reply was loud and sharp, "I can only pick her up on Thursday, and we have to leave immediately to come home, so I'm picking her up at school." The phone went dead. My heart was racing, and sweat formed on my forehead. I knew in my mind there was nothing I could do.

On Thursday morning, I said my goodbyes to Jennifer. She was going to school, and then she would be gone. What she had in her backpack was all she would be taking to Idaho. Jane never allowed Jennifer to bring things from my house to hers, and she only allowed her the clothes she was wearing when she visited me.

I went to work and kept busy all day. At lunch, I stopped and thought about how she would not be home from school, and a tear formed in my eye. Around 3:00, I found myself wanting to go to Jennifer's school and pick her up. That had been a part of my day every day for months. I pulled over to the side of the road and honored how much I was going to miss seeing her.

I had dinner with Sheila and was preoccupied with thoughts of how Jennifer was doing. I did not sleep well that night. I did not want to go home. I just wanted to survive the night and not feel how much I was going to miss Jennifer.

I woke early on Friday and waited until noon to call Jane's number. Jennifer answered. She seemed happy to be with her dog, mom, and Brent, Jane's husband. She said, "I have my own room with my own TV and a new canopy bed." She continued, "You know my mom left my trampoline in Bozeman." She seemed excited, happy, and glad to be in Idaho. She said her mom was at work, and I told her we would come visit as soon as we could and hung up.

I knew Jennifer was fine, and I was so grateful for the opportunity to have spent the past few months with her. I felt I had received a gift that was a miracle. I also felt I had bonded with Jennifer at a level that would last forever. During the past four months, we had become father and daughter. Something new existed for me, the love a parent has for a child, the love a father has for a daughter.

There was something more in life that I wanted. Something real. All my life I had experiences that I could relate to something artificial: drugs, women, money, sex. The list goes on and on. But what I was experiencing with Jennifer was so different. I could not explain the unexplainable. I wanted more of it.

Later that month, Sheila and I had a ceremony in which we committed ourselves to each other. I gave up my apartment and moved in with her. We agreed to create a space just for me. Space, how important that is to my survival. We took an old house out behind hers, and I gutted it, creating a beautiful large room with a raised ceiling, wood floors, new sheet rock, a new door, and a large window. I spent three of the happiest months of my life working on that building. It gave me a sense of accomplishment and satisfaction to have created a special place for me. It was perfect. The large window was over the area for my desk. I had an unobstructed view of a mountain. It was completely built with my own hands. I created a sitting area with a television and stereo. The room enjoyed an abundance of natural light.

I continued in my commitment to recovery. I joined my friend Leslie in starting a "men's group." Attendance was poor, without much commitment. Then I met Robert Johnson, a self-proclaimed psychic, and we started "The Men's Wisdom Council." It was a great success right away. Over the period of a year we met weekly. Eventually it was only ten men coming regularly, and we moved the meetings to one man's house and set them for every other Friday.

My space was completed by fall. I remembered the instructions from the last day at the Hoffman Institute: "Your homework is to totally love and accept your parents, unconditionally." I talked to my mom at Christmas and suggested that she come and visit in the summer. She said she would love to visit Montana.

I planned a get-together of all my friends. It would be a potluck picnic. I was excited by the idea of having my mom here with just me. There would be no competing with my brothers and sisters for her attention. I still hated her for not protecting me when I was young, but this was a new day and I wanted to show her I was worth knowing. My actions all screamed, "Look Mom, I turned out all right."

The visit was all about impressing her. "Look Mom, I have lots of friends. Look Mom, I have a beautiful partner. Look Mom, I am a nice guy." This was her first visit to my life, and I wanted her to like me and want me for a son.

It was the perfect visit. Marian and her sister attended the party. Dozens of people stopped by. It was all natural and relaxing. The image I projected for my mom to see was everything I wanted and nothing I didn't. There were no disasters. The sun was shining brightly on me.

I had finally made it. I had a great job, a mom who thought I was valuable, a woman who loved me, and I was a loving father. I contacted the last few people I owed money to from the divorce and made arrangements to pay them off.

Fall arrived, and Eddie invited Sheila and me to join the family on a seven-day cruise, even offering to pay our way. Eddie and Al would be there with their wives, Jenny and her husband, Dee, and Mom. Sheila and I agreed to spend a week on a ship in the ocean with my family.

We had never been a family by any definition of mine. The week flew by with meals, shows, partying, and shopping. I enjoyed the surface relationships, but a part of me was hoping for more. I was still so afraid of all of them. I kept a safe distance from them for myself.

The following summer, Mom came to visit again for a few weeks. We talked for hours. She clearly remembered everything about when I was growing up. She confirmed beliefs I carried about myself, my father, my siblings, and her. I asked questions, and she offered incredible insights into my past and present. The things I learned from her were not available from any other human on the planet. She was fun and easy to be around. Here was a woman I had never known, and now I found so much in common with her. Having her completely to myself was powerful beyond belief. I was special in my mom's eyes.

I was able to be honest and forthcoming with my thoughts, beliefs, and feelings. She was so innocent I could no longer hold any anger against her. I found myself creating an image of a mom, and this image was unique and different, unlike any I had ever known or conceived.

I was getting ahead financially. I purchased an old mobile home and moved it onto an empty lot belonging to Sheila. I was starting to look ahead and build myself an investment for the future. Working fulltime consumed the best hours of my day. The rest were spent on projects. My job was secure, yet I focused on worrying about getting ahead. I always had a crisis to focus on, responding to whatever fire was burning the most out of control. It was easy and natural for me.

I believed that once a year I needed to do something to keep the healing of my life going. That fall I discovered Haven, a retreat center for healing, and chose a "Come Alive" workshop to attend. I continually listened to people who were working on changing their lives and always seemed to find the right place to go for the next level in my healing process.

One day in August, the phone rang. It was Jane. "Jennifer is going to live with you 'til I can move up there," she said. There was anger in her voice.

My stomach went totally hollow. I tried to breathe, but it was impossible. "What?" I squeezed through my lips.

"I want you to meet me halfway today. I've had all I can take. Jennifer will have to stay with you until I can move up there."

Everything was happening way too fast for me to sort through it. I did not have time for a defense, so I simply said, "Okay, I will leave in fifteen minutes and meet you halfway on the road." It was a hard four-hour drive on two-lane mountain roads, so I asked Sheila to join me. We left right away. There was the excitement of Jennifer moving back to Bozeman, and then there was the confusion and questions over what was going on. Why the emergency?

I could see the little car coming down the highway. I guessed it was Jane. She pulled over, and I could see right away she was upset. The way she pulled Jennifer's bags from the trunk indicated this was not a safe place for me, let alone Jennifer. She said she would see Jennifer in a few weeks.

It was a long ride back to Bozeman. Jennifer seemed to be more comfortable than anyone. She said, "I want to live in Bozeman and go to school there." She explained that she and her mom had been fighting for days about it, and her mom had given in and agreed it would be best for Jennifer to live in Montana.

It was a month before the start of school. I called the school, and yes, they would welcome Jennifer back. It was all set. I knew I must be doing something right, because the disasters in my life were becoming rewarding instead of devastating. I was dealing with my feelings of fear and anxiety.

Jennifer fit perfectly into our family. She was happy to be back. She missed her mom but knew Jane would be moving to Bozeman in a month, too. A month went by, then we were told it would be two. Jane finally arrived just before Christmas. She and Jennifer moved into the old family home. Jennifer had everything she'd always wanted, both of her parents in the same town at the same time.

It was short-lived. Jane's behavior was wild and threatening. It was only three weeks before she called and said, "Come get your daughter and her stuff." She had decided she would have to return to Sun Valley, and Jennifer would stay with us until school was out.

We arrived to find Jennifer sitting in the front yard crying. Jane was yelling and throwing things. She had literally thrown Jennifer's belongings out on the front lawn. She was yelling about how bad Bozeman was as I loaded Jennifer's things into my car. I wiped Jennifer's tears and told her, "It will be all right. Your mom is just mad. She'll get over it."

Over the next couple of months, things got totally out of hand. Jane would call Jennifer and threaten to take her to Sun Valley if she didn't like the way Jennifer talked. Jennifer was in fourth grade. During second and third grade in Sun Valley, she'd attended a private Christian School with only fifteen students. Jennifer wanted to attend public school, and her mom refused. So, both being very strong-willed, the fight was on. Jennifer finally won and moved to Montana to attend a school she liked, even at the cost of not being with her mom.

Jane's threats scared Jennifer. On one particular occasion, Jane told Jennifer that she would be here in a few days to pick her up and Jennifer would never see me again.

I explained to Jennifer that it was not right, and I could stop it, but once I started it would mean that Jennifer would have to live in Montana by my rules. She could choose to live with her mom anytime, but she could not change schools during any school year. I told her, "I will arrange it so all future decisions of where you live will be up to me, and your mom will stop threatening you."

On another front, I had begun to feel the need to challenge myself. I offered to all the men in my group that I would start a small group with the purpose of being closer and more intimate. Three men expressed interest, and we set the first meeting date. During the next couple of months, four of us met once a week. Walter, John and I were committed, but every few weeks the fourth member left the group for one reason or another. We played basketball and then talked about the experience each of us had. We went to a strip club and then talked about our experience. We cooked together and talked about our experience. Finally, after months of doing a number of different activities together, we decided that starting a business together would bring up "issues" for each of us to deal with.

I had a friend, David, who manufactured plastic items like brochure holders, cardholders, and the like. He also sold custom-cut plastic signs to my employer. One afternoon while picking up an order for the sign company, I asked if he had run across any good business ideas. Now, David reminded me of the absent-minded professor. He took me in the back of the showroom and handed me a small, white 2-ounce bottle with a yellow label. It was labeled "CD Repair." In talking with him, I learned of his experience and dream of marketing it. He said he had given up and was open to any ideas or offers.

At the next group meeting, I shared with Walter and John the opportunity I saw in this product. They agreed to investigate it with me, but both were very cautious. It seemed that I had made lots of assumptions about what others agreed to and didn't agree to. I heard the answers I wanted to hear and did not listen to what others were saying. So, the first few meetings where we talked about the new project were tough for me. I had an agenda, and John and Walter were holding me back from getting what I wanted. I wanted them to go along with me on this adventure.

We met with David a few times and decided to go ahead with the business. We were all clear about our intention, to use the business as a tool to create intimacy between us.

Things really started moving forward. I was working to have a successful project and soon lost sight of the objective of intimacy. I could smell the money, fame, and fortune. Oh, I was back in the game of "get rich quick." Over the months, I fought with Walter and John over integrity, success, and being right.

To stop Jane from threatening Jennifer, I hired an attorney, Paul Smart. I sought him out because he had a reputation for family law and getting things done. He was expensive and required a large retainer. After reviewing the case, he made several suggestions that I agreed to. He filed a motion for a new parenting plan and a temporary order for Jennifer to remain in the state of Montana while the final plan was worked out.

I totally caught Jane by surprise. All of a sudden, the shoe was on the other foot. Jane would have to answer to a judge before just taking Jennifer anywhere. I refused to speak directly with Jane. Each time she called she was verbally out of control. She was beyond mad. She was making lots of threats. She could visit Jennifer under written agreement only.

Summer arrived, and she took Jennifer to a Bible retreat and spent time with her, returning her as agreed.

Jennifer was happier than I had seen her. She had more loving attention from her mom than she had received in the past year, and now her mom was mad at me and not her. Jennifer was on a basketball team, playing the flute, and getting straight A's in school. I was a very proud father.

For me, standing up to Jane and saying "enough is enough" was rewarding and   another mile marker on the road to recovering my life. My confidence was strong and I had the support of Sheila and my friends. I had enough money to afford to fight Jane. I was afraid, more frightened than I could remember ever being, but I had a support team to help me when I felt the world closing in. That November, four years after our commitment ceremony, Sheila and I were married.

Things started to move ahead with our CD scratch remover company, Dizzy Brothers. We worked out a deal with Hastings Entertainment, a small Texas company that had over a hundred stores.   One was in Bozeman, and there were several in surrounding towns. Walter, John, and I were magic together. Walter established a relationship with the store managers that got us the opportunity to sell our product in the local stores. We then worked for months trying to convince corporate Hastings of our value and success. No one listened. Between Thanksgiving and Christmas, we had product in six of their stores, and sales were through the roof. Still no one was listening.

In January 1999, Walter, John, and I were exhausted and not getting anywhere with marketing the scratch remover nationally. We were having explosive discussions, and Walter and John were learning they had to stand up to me or I would bulldoze right over them. I was all out for healing what kept me separated from others, especially men, but money was more important. It was the answer to all my prayers. If I just made it rich, I would be "fixed." Walter and John did not agree with me on the future of the business. They were satisfied with things the way they were and were interested in the intimacy aspect of our group.

On the final day, when we were going to throw in the towel, Katie, a new buyer for Hastings, agreed to buy our product and place it in all of their stores. There were a few glitches, but I was sure it would work. I presented the glitches to Walter and John, and their lack of excitement killed me. I was angry and hurt that they would stand in the way of my success. They went along with selling to Hastings, but questioned the focus of our group. "Is it mostly about money or about relationships?" they asked. "Are we giving up some of our principles?" I couldn't see their point; money was a much grander point.

The order was placed, the product shipped, and we were on our way. The first few months required keeping track of sales and getting reports from Hastings. They seemed to be a very disorganized company. It was frustrating to deal with. We hung in there and worked each problem out, all the time having meetings to discuss our different opinions. I felt Walter and John were holding me back, and they expressed concerns for my objectivity and integrity. I finally had something that was working, and I'd be damned if I was going to let them destroy it.

I learned a lot from working with Walter and John. I would get very angry and hang up on three-way phone calls without saying a word. I gradually learned from them to inform people about what was up for me. Working with them was a huge challenge. With the focus being on our relationship and not the business, things never seemed to go the way I thought they should.

More and more, I wanted out. We talked about selling my share and then about selling the business. We eventually had the company appraised. I was barely able to talk with Walter or John without getting angry. I saw a gold mine, and they were never going to let me find the gold. Looking back, it was similar to my experience with Satellite Control and many other projects in my life, except this time I hung in there and did not allow my anger to destroy everything.

Summer arrived, and Jane wrote to say she would be picking Jennifer up to attend the summer Bible camp again. It was a Friday in early July. I helped Jennifer load her things into Jane's truck. Jane was different, but I didn't pay much attention. She seemed to be nervous, or edgy, just different than usual. She was to return Jennifer on Monday.

When darkness fell Monday night, I began to have an uneasy feeling. When they still weren't back by midnight, I called Jane's number in Idaho, knowing her husband was home. The machine finally picked it up. I left a message, but something was out of place. I knew Brent should be home. I left a clear message saying I was very worried that Jennifer and Jane had not returned from Bible camp. I ended with, "Please call immediately."

By morning, my mind was going crazy considering all the possibilities. Brent not returning my call was puzzling and suspicious. It kept lurking in the back of my mind. At 9:00 am I called my attorney. He said until I found them there was nothing that could be done. About 1:30 pm I called Jane's home phone number again. This time I left the message, "Brent, please call me. I am very worried about Jane and Jennifer. I have called the police to file a missing persons report." Suddenly I heard a click in the phone and knew someone was picking up the line. Jane's words were clear and sharp, "We are fine," and the line went dead. I knew it. And that was all I needed to get me going.

I called my attorney and set up a meeting. He told me we would need a physical address where we could serve Jane. All I had was a Post Office box number. The phone number was unlisted, so I contacted a friend who was able to turn any phone number into an address. My attorney was excellent at dealing with it. Within a couple of days, he had the sheriff in Idaho serve Jane with papers requiring her to return Jennifer immediately or face prosecution. I went to the police and was in the process of filing criminal charges when I received a call saying that Jane had called and would return Jennifer the next day.

How do you spell victory? Picking Jennifer up at Jane's newest attorney's office was scary and at the same time empowering. The judge issued me full temporary custody. So, until he decided differently, Jennifer would live with me.

I was on top of the world. This was beyond healing. It was justice. Even with my ego flying high, I knew I must keep my cool and continue my act. I had won this battle, but the war was not over.

The summer was long, and the attorneys seemed to be the only ones winning. They were mediating our "parenting plan." Mine would be the primary household for the first year, and so it would continue until Jane and I agreed on something different. Basically, I had complete say over where Jennifer lived forever.

Jennifer was no longer wanting to live with Sheila and me. She was upset that her mom was being devastated by my actions, and she started lobbying for living with her mom. I agreed under the condition she would finish the school year here.

Selling signs, parenting Jennifer full time, fighting for her freedom, being in business with two partners, and being in a relationship with Sheila were not enough. I decided that I would purchase more mobile homes and remodel them to increase my income and create some long-term investments. Selling signs was financially rewarding and fun. The business with my partners, Dizzy Brothers, was earning each of us the equivalent of a fulltime income with virtually no time required. I was extremely busy and playing at the top of my game. I worked from early morning until I fell asleep.

The summer sped by. Jennifer, business, work, and Sheila. In July, Jennifer moved to Idaho to live with her mom. On Labor Day weekend, we traveled to the Oregon coast with Sheila's brother and sister-in-law. We joined Sheila's son Timmy and his girlfriend Judy for a weekend of relaxing on the beach and car racing. It was an incredible weekend of campfires, walking on the beach, great food, and wonderful company. Life had never been this good.

It had been 16 years since I started working on myself, beginning with counseling after divorcing Marian. I had worked with private therapists, in groups, and in workshops, and I had explored my childhood intensely.

I'd found places where I was valued, and worked with supportive friends to help each other deal with the pain we felt in our lives. Some groups had tried to force change, while others had opened my eyes to healing with love and attention. Some had given me a place to belong, rules to practice, friends, and hope for a way out of my trouble. Others had helped me practice unconditional love. I benefited from the practical tools I'd learned for crisis management and anger management. I eventually learned that I had to teach what I really wanted to learn and live, and I had started groups of my own. I had gathered supportive people around me who helped me with my life.

I was looking for more than being able to cope. I wanted to be "fixed" forever. I was committed to fixing myself and never quitting until I was sure I would never put myself in a violent situation again. It had been 10 years since I put the gravel through Jane's windshield, and I had not committed an act of violence or destruction since.

I had climbed to the top of the heap. I was in control. Power and control were what had gotten me in trouble in the past, and they were what saved me. Through techniques and willpower, I was keeping myself in check. I was busy, happy, and successful. It took energy, but God was finally giving me access to the good things other people got from life.

I had a feeling inside that it all took too much energy, and I worried that everything was an act. It was a great act, and I liked the act I had created: healing, love, support, and moving ahead. It was my baby. But I felt it was an act, nonetheless. I had done enough work to be able to function in the world, and I was resigned to thinking that was the way life was.

I didn't realize I was still living in the dark. And I had no idea day was about to break.

The Awakening

September 12, 2000 was, in fact, a beautiful day. Sheila and I had been looking forward to this evening for weeks. We would be attending a Rebirthing Workshop which had been suggested by Renee and Linda, our massage therapists.

Rebirthing is a simple breathing technique that is used to release unexpressed emotions. It can help to release stress, anger, sadness, and feelings connected to one's self worth. It can expand consciousness, making one aware of limiting patterns and beliefs and reconnecting one with the Source.

My life was very busy. I pretty much thought I had everything under control. I earned enough money and had investments for the future, so financially I was confident. I got a massage every week, a four-handed massage, not just the ordinary kind. I was in control and winning at the game of life.

I was excited by any idea that would fix Sheila. I did not really need any of this for myself. I had been working on myself for years. I would attend just to be supportive of Sheila. She was excited about doing this work.

The session was led by a woman named Victoria. We lay down on floor pads and had nice blankets to cover with. We started a deep breathing exercise. I enjoyed relaxing and escaping the worries of the day.

The music was loud with a deep bass beat to it. As I listened to the drums, breathing deeper and deeper, something started to happen. It was like stepping into a dream. I found myself getting confused, yet with a sense of freedom. I thought, "What the hell am I doing?"

The answer was immediate, "I am in control." My coach, Roger, was telling me to keep breathing. I relaxed and could feel myself drifting through many scenes, some familiar, some unknown. I was drifting in a dream world.

All of a sudden, my body was wracked with pain. My first reaction was to avoid it. What a weird dream. I was pregnant and about to give birth to a baby boy. But the pain. Oh, God, I had never felt such pain. Where was I? Who was I? Inside my head, I was screaming, "WHAT THE HELL HAVE YOU DONE?" I was having trouble concentrating on my breathing. The pain came in waves, and with each wave I kept pushing and pushing. Suddenly there was nothing, not a sound, just silence. In the silence I heard a voice in my head say, "The baby is dead..."

Another voice spoke quietly in the distance, "Lee, Lee." Then louder, "Lee. It's time to return." I did not recognize the voice, but it seemed to know me. I turned to see where it was coming from, and poof, I was out of the dream. I took a deep breath and opened my eyes fully. Roger was there.

"The baby is dead," I whispered. "You know what? The baby is dead..." Suddenly I was awake and confused. Had I just experienced giving birth to a baby, and the baby was dead?

For the rest of the night I was absorbed with thoughts of the dead baby. Something about it was unsettling. There was a loss of control that accompanied the experience. I could count on one hand the number of times I had lost control of my life. I don't mean the ordinary common loss of control. I mean the strength, training, and conviction that it takes to control a bowel movement. It was as though I had crapped my pants. I have practiced controlling myself to the extent that I am always in control. And that night I had lost control.

The next day, I had scheduled a Rotary luncheon and then a massage. Normally, my massages were at 1:30 in the afternoon, but today 6:00 pm was the only time available. I hated Rotary. I felt so inferior to all the people in there. Being in their presence reminded me of how phony I was. I decided to skip Rotary and had lunch with Sheila instead. It was a great day. A little shopping, no work, just a day of fun.

I arrived for the massage a few minutes early. Lying on the table, I was suddenly wracked with pain again. Naked and confused, I wondered what the hell was happening to me. I couldn't stand the pain in my gut. I sat up with the blanket wrapped around me. Renee and Linda both tried to comfort me. One moment the sweat was pouring from my body, soaking the sheets and blankets, and the next I was freezing.

"What can we do?" they asked. "Should we call Victoria?" They were both composed. What should I do? Should I go to the hospital? Or should I hang tough and see my way through this? The pain was growing. It was worse than I believed I had ever felt. But worse than that, my mind was running wild, wondering what I had gotten myself into. I could shut off the pain but not my mind.

This was a small office on the fifth floor of an ancient office building. Adjoining offices were filled with counselors, realtors, and lawyers. I wondered if they could hear me. What were Linda and Renee thinking? Was I scaring them? Oh yes, the pain was overtaking my mind, screaming for attention, "GOD HELP ME." "You'd better call Victoria and tell her that the dead baby is back," I said. "Tell her to hurry. I don't know how long I can hang on." Back to the pain. Holy shit, this was getting out of hand. I knew it would go away. I could control it.

It had been almost half an hour. "What time is it?" I asked. My God, time had stopped. Yes, I knew it had only been a couple of minutes since I last asked. Am I going crazy? Is the pain getting worse? What a great time for my body to crap out. What are people going to say? Shit, I can't have firemen and paramedics seeing me here in this condition.

"Don't call an ambulance," I said. "I'll be fine. Where's Victoria? Did she say she was coming? Did you tell her to hurry?" My God, what was wrong? Why wasn't she here? Didn't she know how much I needed her help?

What a day, what a month. I had earned more money than I had ever thought possible. I had closed the biggest deal of my career. People liked me. I was appreciated and valued. I was on top of the world, and I had gotten there on my own. I had done everything, everything, to change who I was. I had worked hard, memorizing how to think, feel, behave, talk, dress, smell, believe, and act, how to show my heart just enough to get what I wanted. I was good. So, someone please explain to me what the hell was happening to me.

"Maybe you'd better call an ambulance," I said. "This seems to be getting worse. Must be something I ate." If I kept talking, it would be all right. Keep moving, keep thinking, keep avoiding the pain, it would go away. "Don't feel the pain, it will kill you," I heard from deep within myself.

I kept flashing to all the scenes in my life that involved pain. This pain was outdoing all of them. When it came to separating myself from pain, I was the king. My mind continued to dance, looking for the memory that would let me know I had survived worse, but the pain kept pulling me back to the present.

I could remember all the times my father yanked me, hit me, humiliated me, whipped me, knocked me down, broke my head open with his cane. The parade of memories seemed endless. I could not understand how this pain could be so much greater. My childhood contained memories of pain that had never been measured, but now I was measuring them, comparing each and every one to the pain now running through my body. None compared. They only confirmed that I was in trouble, big trouble.

When does recovery start? What is hitting bottom? How many times can you hit bottom? When will it end? Did it start with the prayer I made when I was a little boy? How deep is this hell I have created?

What? The ambulance? Oh shit, firemen. By this time, I had my boxers on. The pain was completely consuming my being. The sad thing about being in control was that the mind thought of everything. I wished I didn't weigh so much. It was going to be no picnic getting me down five flights of stairs.

"Just give me something to stop the pain," I said. The pain was getting harder and harder to escape. If I surrendered, I would die.

I was asked to lie down on the stretcher. "Can you give me something to stop the pain?" I kept repeating, asking quietly at first, then louder and louder. I listened to them discuss my situation and answered lots of questions. No, I had not taken any drugs. I had not eaten since lunch. No, no, no. I had done nothing. I closed my eyes. I could stand no more. Maybe if I closed my eyes I would wake up from this nightmare.

The ride to the first floor was beyond my ability to comprehend. Lights, noise, and voices all blending together while the pain had totally consumed my body. I could no longer think. "Can you give me something?" I asked. "This really hurts. Please help me." I was offering anything and everything as a hope of escaping the overwhelming pain. It was like making a deal with God. I knew they could help me, but nothing I did was getting me the relief I needed.

The ride to the hospital seemed unreal. The sounds of the sirens, the voices on the radios, the vibration from the road, the smell of exhaust, people talking about me and me understanding everything that was going on, yet as though I were someone else. All the time remembering, "I am in control. I know what I am doing. I can get them to fix me. It is not that big of a deal."

"Just give me something for the pain," I demanded. "I cannot handle the pain." Talking, screaming, demanding, begging, nothing seemed to work. It seemed like forever. Suddenly, I recognized Sheila's voice. She would help me. "Sheila, tell them I need drugs."

When I woke up, the room was dark. I could make out a man in a white coat standing by my bed. "Are you the doctor?" I asked and waited for a reply.

"Yes, I'm your doctor," he said. His voice sounded cold and uncaring, and it scared me. I knew I had information he needed to be aware of. I didn't even have to think about it.

"Look Doc, there's more going on here than just my physical illness. Did anyone tell you about the dead baby?" There was no response from him, so I continued, "A couple of days ago I went to a workshop with my wife. It was this new age thing called a Rebirthing. It was very intense, and that's when I first felt the pain in my stomach. Everything's starting to make sense now. I gave birth to a dead baby."

My senses and his lack of response were telling me that I sounded like some kind of drugged up idiot. "Look, I know what happened to me," I said. "I need you to understand that this is about the dead baby. It's about my whole life. I need you to listen."

The morphine was taking its toll on my ability to communicate, but still, how could I trust a doctor who would not listen? My body felt stiff, protective. The pain was gone, but there were new feelings, sheer panic, absolute loss of control.

I began to believe I had been captured and put in a prison where they were doing experiments. I had to find someone to help me get out of there. My mind kept flashing from one scene to another, doctors, nurses, visitors all blending together with childhood scenes. Nothing seemed real, and yet I thought everything was real and happening to me.

As each of my friends visited, I found them to be uncooperative in seeing what was happening. I trusted no one. Every day my will to fight was weakening. On the seventh day, I listened to the conversations going on around me. So, there was nothing more they could do for me or to me.

Suddenly, Sheila was there, thank God. I was sure she had abandoned me. "Hi," slowly found its way out of my lips. It was my body that had failed me. Inside, everything was clear and real, yet trying to communicate was nearly impossible. "I just want to go home," I said. The words were difficult. The smile on her face went straight to my heart. Everything would be all right, just a little time. I saw lights flashing above my head as we traveled down a hall. Where were we going?

The doctors had said there was nothing more they could do for me in Bozeman. The only hope for my recovery was to send me to Seattle. As the ambulance pulled away from the hospital, I felt a sense of relief. Finally, I was out of the control of a bunch of crazy people. As I drifted in and out of consciousness, I was aware that I had completed my tour of hell.

When we arrived at the airport, everything seemed like it was happening to someone else, not me. As I looked around the plane, and saw Sheila sitting on the other side, I knew things would be all right. I knew she would not let them hurt me. It was okay to let go and sleep. The plane was cold and noisy, yet sleep seemed easy. I was safe.

I could hear the tires screeching as the plane touched down. I opened my eyes, and I saw Sheila still sitting across from me. She was all I could see from my position. As they transferred me to the ambulance, the sky was a beautiful blue. There was dampness in the air. The sun was warm on my face, and I could hear voices all around me. Everything danced around me, magically entertaining me. It was as though a large dark cloud had been lifted from my life. I knew I was going to live. Now, to deal with how I felt about it.

I had suffered a pancreatic attack. I learned that I had chronic pancreatitis. It's an inflammatory disease that causes progressive, irreversible damage to the pancreas. In about 30% of cases, including mine, there is no known cause.

MRI's showed that 90% of my pancreas had been destroyed. My doctor determined that the best approach would be to wait and let my body wall off that portion of the pancreas and rebuild my strength. So the only answer was pain control and time.

My world had become small. Nothing outside of the hospital room existed. The room was a pale blue, and one wall was all windows with a breathtaking view of Seattle. There was a faint smell of sewage in the air. My room was the last one at the end of the hall. I loved being in what appeared to be the quiet area of this floor.

I couldn't believe Sheila was still here. I wondered if it was possible that she really cared about me? I was too tired to think about it and just wanted to check out for a while.

When I opened my eyes, I saw the largest bouquet of flowers I had ever seen. The smell of the flowers filled the air. How beautiful! Sheila walked across the room and handed me the card. It was from my brothers and father. It was a first class showing of their concern for my illness. "How dare they send me these flowers," I thought, "to pretend they really cared." My energy was low, and I did not have time to think about it. The task at hand was what was going to happen to me.

Every day the interns checked on me. Some days I saw a doctor. The nurses were kind and gentle. I just wanted to know what to expect. How long would I be here? What was it going to take for me to be well? No one seemed to have answers.

Sheila arrived every morning and spent the day with me. She stayed until late into the evening. It was only a few days before I was able to get up and take short walks with an IV bag on a stand and tubes hanging out of me. There were periodic MRI scans. I thought I would die when they stuck me in that machine. Anxiety filled my whole being.

And there were the nights. I would get so overwhelmed with anxiety that I could not go to sleep. Drugs were the only thing that helped me through those moments of pain and fear. I trusted nothing and nobody. Even the nurses were suspect. There was one male nurse named Bill who was very patient with me. He always did what he said he would. I felt he really cared and understood how frightened I was.

After my childhood, with no control over what was happening to me, I was freaking out. Here I was again with no control. And again I knew I could trust NOBODY except myself. I tested everyone, and as each day passed, I found the limits of how much I could trust each new person in my life: doctors, nurses, aides, and even Sheila. My body had rebelled against me, and I did not know anything except that I was in serious trouble and alone.

Before I went into the hospital, I had three wishes for my life. The first was to lose weight, the second was to be able to forgive my father, and the third was to be known as a kind, gentle, loving man. Through the pain and fear of my illness, through the total loss of control of my body and everything around me, I gradually came to understand that my wishes were coming true.

I have known myself as fat and ugly all my life. I have always believed that if I just weighed less life would be easier. My weight has always been proof that there was something wrong with me that everyone could see. In the secrecy of my mind, I would make promises and deals with God. If I were just slim, then I could do and be everything I wanted. I lost 50 pounds during my hospitalization, and to me this was the answer to one of my lifelong prayers. It was a blessing and one of the rewards of being sick.

Since attending the Hoffman Institute, I knew that forgiving and unconditionally accepting and loving my parents was another obstacle between me and the life I wanted. I felt burdened by being the victim of my father's abuse, and I wanted to be free of that burden. I had prayed and thought about how my inability to see my father in a different light was keeping me from all that was possible for me. It had been seven years since I came to believe that was what lay between me and my happiness. I would have given anything to find my way through this. ANYTHING.

One night I was lying in the hospital alone and had a vision. I traveled out of the room in a blue light. I felt like I went halfway and met a twelve-year-old boy. I visited and played on logs with him and found him to be fun, creative, intelligent, loving, and caring. At some point I realized that he was my father before his accident. It was his smile, the wink of his eye, and the way he tilted his head that first gave it away. But then he said, "How do you know?" The curiosity and the way he said it was the clincher. He was my father before the accident. I had never considered him as anything other than a mean, harsh, and unhappy human being. In that moment, I opened a place in my heart for him. This was the true healing I had been searching for.

My third wish, to be known as a kind, gentle, loving man, came from something I had once read on a park bench while waiting for a ferry. I was traveling by myself, and when I read the plaque on the back of the bench, I knew it was how I wanted my epitaph to read, "A kind, gentle, loving man." Something clicked inside me. This was it. This was what I really wanted, really, really, really wanted. I had never been so clear about what I was willing to give my life for. This was it, the final piece of the puzzle. No matter what was to happen, this was where I wanted to be when I died.

This time the prayer was different. The idea of being known as a gentle, kind, loving man was so far beyond anything I could ever imagine in my life, I said a silent and secret prayer, the kind Grandma used to say. "A kind, gentle, loving man is how I want to be known. I will give anything, absolutely anything including my life, to be that."

During my illness, there was love all around me. There were people praying for me and for my life every day. People called. They sent cards. Over 70 people sent cards at one point. It was the caring of other people that challenged my belief that nobody cared. That had been the theme of my life, and now it was challenged. I had wanted to feel this love all my life, and now lying there in the hospital bed, there was nothing else. I was surrounded by love and acceptance at a time when I had nothing. I had nothing to give.

My heart opened to the overwhelming outpour of support and love that I received from all the people in my life. It was like a cold, hard rock that melted under the enormous amount of love I received. Kindness and love began to grow in me. There was a sense that I was on my way to a better place. I hung onto life because for the first time in my life I knew what I wanted to be when I grew up, and it seemed to be within my grasp, a "kind, gentle, loving man."

I should have lost everything I owned. My father was about my age when he had the perforated ulcer. He did lose everything, his wife, children, friends, and money. He is now living in a camping trailer in an old trailer court in Las Vegas. He is still in control of his life.

For me, the baby is dead. I was forced to give up control and drop the act of my "successful" life. I let go of everything and found that I was being held. My wishes were coming true.

Being so sick, unable to do anything for myself, I knew that I was getting what I wished for and that I was at the mercy of a power greater than me. I had no choice but to trust, because I knew I was not in control. Simple things like brushing my teeth were almost impossible. I had no power and no control of anything or anyone, not even myself.

My illness was a gift. Even today, and every day, when I give up control and spread love to those around me, I receive back the gift of a loving, meaningful life. It took me months in the hospital, recovering at home, and trying to step back into life before I fully realized the truth of what I was being shown.

I awoke each morning seeking answers about my health. When would I be all right? When would I be able to eat? Every question contained WHEN. Yes, I would survive and be fully functional someday. It was up to my body. We would just have to wait and see how each day went.

I was shocked to wake up every day and find Sheila sitting beside my bed. I thought, "What the hell is she doing here? She should be gone by now. I'm sure she has more important things to do." It didn't matter that we were married and had been committed to each other for over six years. I felt she should have left me. The truth for me had been that nobody really cared that much. I was used to people who only cared about themselves, and I'd always believed that was why Sheila was with me, because of what she got. While I was in the hospital, there was nothing I could give her, and she was still there.

Sheila would explore the hospital with me. It was difficult to walk, but getting out of my room and away from the three channels on the TV was worth it. I loved going to the cafeteria and watching Sheila eat. I was so weak and fragile, yet determined to find things I could do. I felt so lucky to have someone there with me every day. So many people in the hospital seemed to be alone. The man next door was told he only had weeks to live. His attitude was amazing. He looked at me and said, "They did what they could," and went on to say, "I have appreciated living, and I am going to continue to appreciate all that life gives me."

When I wasn't feeling sorry for myself or finding some other way to distract myself, I was entertained by other patients. One was Annie. She had been a country singer. For Halloween, she had decorated her IV stand with scraps of paper and an old orange bag with a pumpkin on it. She would go up and down the hall singing and talking to everyone who would listen. How could she have such a terrible life and be so happy? I would hear her in the hall and get dressed and join her. I listened to her stories of adventure and disappointment. Yet through it all I could clearly see that she had nothing but her attitude and those old memories. Here I was, younger, healthier, better off financially, and not alone, yet my attitude was one of disappointment, resentment, and seeing myself a victim.

There was another woman who had a sister from Montana. As I got to know them, I found they were sweet, kind, and surrounded by family. Each day when I walked, I would stop for a few minutes and visit with them. She had a terrible infection in her foot. She had undergone surgery and was recovering. Then one day she was gone. I asked around about her and was sad to discover the surgery had not gotten all the poison. They had had to remove her entire leg, and she had been moved to another floor. I was shocked. The playing field had been leveled in this hospital. Clothes, money, position, none of it made a difference in the struggle against whatever disease each of us faced. My heart went out to each of the people I met. My mind worked hard at sorting out what was happening and why. It was more than I could process, and I was overwhelmed.

One day I was told I could go home to Sheila's son Timmy's house in Seattle. All they needed to do was insert a feeding tube. Getting out of the hospital sounded so good that the idea of sticking a tube through my nose and into my intestines seemed minor. Besides, I would have lots of drugs to remove me from the experience. Drugs, I loved drugs. Everything frightened me, and drugs were the answer to escape the pain and fear.

It was a long ride to Timmy's house, and I felt every bump in the road. The sound of the truck tires on the freeway was so different than any of the sounds in the hospital, I was glad to be hearing it.

We settled into Timmy's house. Judy and Timmy had been living together for a few months. Upon arrival, I questioned Judy about how she justified her and her daughter living with Timmy, when they were not married. Things were already tense between them, and this was just the shove she needed to move on. I knew that I was not comfortable with her ways and hoped she would choose to spend more time with her mom, which she did. Sometimes it was fun to control the world around me. I did not consider my rudeness and control to be an issue. I just knew that I could not take living with her and her daughter.

I was sentenced to 20 hours a day of being fed through the tube in my nose. It was much more difficult than I had imagined. The tube was always getting plugged, and I would panic trying to clear it.

I slept on the couch. Timmy made me up a special bed in the living room by the fireplace, but the smell of the ashes made me sick to my stomach. I spent most of my time in the family room in front of the television. Every movement was difficult and demanding.

We had been there about a week when Sheila needed to go home and complete some work. Timmy had a car race to attend in Arizona. I would be alone for a couple of days. I felt that I could easily take care of myself. After all, I was in control.

Since the attack, fear had been totally running my life. I did not feel I was given a choice. Fear was the only choice.

After everyone left, the problems started right away. Of course, the tube became plugged. Then my medicine didn't seem to be relaxing me. The day seemed too long. All I wanted to do was lie down and die. Yet, I was so afraid of the pain that would be associated with dying that I did everything I could to avoid pain. Every hour seemed like a day. I was sweating, then chilled. My stomach was sick. No matter what I tried, I failed. I was sleeping by the fireplace when I started throwing up. I tried to clean up after myself, but the smell was like a refrigerator that had been closed for years and suddenly opened. I was scared but still not out of control. It would be between eight and ten hours before Timmy would return. I would have to make the best of it. Part of my feeding tube had dislodged and come out when I was vomiting. Worst of all was the thought that I was damaging Timmy's house.

I held it together all day. When Timmy came in, I told him I needed to go to the hospital. I started vomiting again, and the tube was creating more vomiting. I grabbed it and pulled it out. I knew I was sick, just not sure how bad it was. We arrived at the emergency room, and after an hour a doctor came to visit and explained that I would not be going home. There was a sense of relief for me. I laid my head back on the pillow and went to sleep. Just before drifting off, I told the doctor that I wanted to be on the tenth floor. Oh, the smell of the hospital, scary but safe.

"We are not going to let you out of here until you're able to eat on your own." The doctor's words rang in my ears. I thought I was safe. I had not made the tenth floor. I was now on the sixteenth floor. New nurses, a totally different staff to deal with. The daytime nurse had a drill instructor's attitude. There was no coddling. Her assistant was even worse. She was obviously of German descent and very demanding, and her bedside manner was that of a prison guard. I was at the mercy of a staff of hard-nosed individuals. I longed for the fun, caring people of the tenth floor, but there was nothing I could do to change my situation. Were they trying to piss me off or what? There would be no special treatment for me on this floor. I was so angry that I worked hard at getting my act together so I could get out of there.

I swear my main nurse and her assistant never took a day off. It was truly the longest three weeks of my life. The cards and letters had slowed down to one a week. The phone calls were better. A couple of friends called every week. Sheila was still there every day. Nothing was quite good enough for me. I worked hard at maintaining control, but with nurses who refused to cooperate, it was nearly impossible.

It was only three weeks before I was eating enough to satisfy the doctors that I could maintain myself over the next couple of months while my body continued to heal. I would be home for Thanksgiving and Christmas. Other than getting an MRI scan every few weeks, I could go home, rebuild my strength, and get ready for surgery in the spring.

Sitting in the living room, rocking in my favorite chair, my spirit was still alive, but I felt totally helpless to control my life. Drugs, drugs, and more drugs. I felt so disconnected from everything that had been important to me. No work, no friends visiting. My life was at a standstill. Everyone seemed so busy.

What had happened to me? I sat and watched television, zoning out, totally in survival mode. I just had to wait for my body to heal. Then there would be surgery. It was as though I were in a bubble. I was just floating along not really connected with anything or able to control anything outside my own mind. My dog "Buddy" sat beside me. I felt he understood my confusion and disconnection from the world. TV was boring. I hated reading. My life was totally out of my control, and that only meant one thing: total annihilation. I just needed to know when it was coming. I would just sit there waiting, rocking and waiting. Some days seemed to last forever. Lost in a meaningless world with no way out, no ability to even think clearly about what was happening, I was at the mercy of drugs and a cruel God.

Surgery was the final part of my healing, or so I thought. When the surgeon came out of the operating room, Sheila was suspicious of his demeanor. Oh, yes it had gone quite well. The gallbladder had been removed, but there had been a lot of damage to the pancreas. Recovery would be a little longer than expected, but I would be fine. Another five months of recovery would be a full year off work. Was I broke? How would we survive? Everything was too much for me to think about. I blocked the questions out of my mind and accepted being at the mercy of something or someone outside myself.

We stayed at Timmy's for a couple more weeks and then returned to Montana for the last of my recovery. None of it was easy or fun. I was on heavy-duty drugs and went through several withdrawals during the first couple of months at home.

As I sat there in the chair for the next five months, I contemplated everything in my life and the meaning it offered.

In June, I started meeting with Walter and John. I no longer wanted to participate in the business. I wanted out. Offers were kicked around, but nothing I felt comfortable with. I felt outgunned by Walter and John and jealous of how well they were getting along with our new manager, Brett. The business was making good money, and I saw potential for much more. I found a buyer who offered $150,000, but they were not selling. Then I approached selling my share to Brett for $40,000. We danced with that idea for months before Brett finally admitted he had too many concerns and other interests.

When I was growing up, Al and Jenny would join sides against me. Whenever I felt that John and Walter were taking sides against me, I would lose control and become angry. Normally, I would be able to use the anger to push my way through to get what I wanted, but my illness, I lacked the energy to fight them and surrendered to their ways. They jokingly offered me $20,000 for my share. I exploded and prepared to defend myself, but in the end, I could only share how hurt I felt.

It was not long before they agreed to sell the business. We talked with Opportunity Training, who had been assisting us with production, about purchasing the business. They made an offer that was reasonable, and on August 1, 2001 they owned the business. It was a win-win deal for both parties. They hired Walter to manage the company, and John and I agreed to advise them at any time for the first two years.

September 13 was my first day back at work. I was up at 4:30 am and ready at 5:30 for the 120-mile drive to Helena and the Monday morning company meeting. I wanted to be there early. Everyone had been so supportive of me while I was sick. Somehow they had managed to find a way to pay me a commission every week but one for an entire year.

I watched the sunrise as I drove through the Townsend Valley and looked over my shoulder to see the moon setting behind me. I pulled over to the side of the road and took a few minutes just to take it all in.

After being gone a year, I was ready to get back to work. I had lost fifty pounds but was already starting to gain it back. First there was the production meeting, then the design meeting. I was amazed that nothing had changed. It was like an old pair of shoes, familiar but different than I remembered.

The drive home was incredibly long. It seemed like everything around me was moving so fast. I was scared of losing what I had found in the past year. I liked being slowed down and more in touch with myself, my body, my needs, my feelings and desires. The fast-paced world of selling signs felt strange. "I will adjust," I told myself, "After all, it has been a year." But something had changed.

The change, what was it? I wanted something different. I wanted to love and be loved. I wanted to be intimate with people. I wanted to be related to others.

Days turned into weeks and weeks into months. I was in constant conflict with myself. I had experienced being out of control for a year, and now I questioned the need to control anything. It was more work holding my life together than I was willing to invest. I found myself confronting the conflict between what was really important to me and what was no longer important. I began to pick and choose what I wanted in my life.

When I reentered my life I saw the difference between the way I was re-entered before and the way I had become. That still keeps me going today, the experience of having no choice, just having to just be in the presence of other people's love for me and not being able to fight against it. I experienced being loved and cared for by people who hardly knew me and by people who knew me too well.

Now that I have re-entered my life, I find that I am softer and more available to love. I am able to recognize my anger, resentments, and frustrations. I get that they are mine and not created by the world around me. They are created by me.

Life seemed short then, and I only wanted to do things that were really important to me. I tried to fit back into my life, but I had become a round peg, and my life was still square. Things that would not have bothered me a year before were now like huge slaps in the face. I was no longer willing to hide my feelings, thoughts, and truths. I also found that I was hearing other people's truths and not liking it. My motto became, "The truth will set you free, but first it will piss you off." I could see with each and every "incident" how I was reacting without thought. I could see that I was the creator of my life.

The past year had opened a view to life that had never existed for me before. I saw choices and possibilities. Being a victim of life was one way to deal with life, but now there was another choice. I could take responsibility for how my life was going.

Being sick for a year gave me the vehicle to see the world I had created. I could see control was a choice. Being a victim was a choice. Everything in my life was a choice. The belief that nobody cared was a choice. I could no longer hide. I could no longer live my life as a tragedy, without taking responsibility for making it a tragedy. God had granted my wishes and given me the gift of my life. It was time for me to give up my act and create a life worthy of those gifts. The baby was dead.

Where to start? Sheila? Yes. Jennifer? Yes. My mom? Yes. My father? ...yes. My brothers, sisters, aunts, uncles? I had been estranged from my family for over 30 years. Now I realized that it had been my choice. And I could choose differently, if I wanted.

The Daily Journey

It has been two years since I went back to work. I gave my notice a few months after returning and completely left work in just over a year. My partners and I sold our business, and I invested in more rentals. I am a student and supporter of Landmark Education. I am aware that I live my life as a response to the past.

As I am cleaning out the closet, I find that writing the story of my life gets me clearly in touch with the lies, secrets, and illusions that I base my future on. I accept responsibility for all my actions and the results in my life. It is a continual process. Every day, I decide if how I am being is worth giving my life to. If it is not, then I look to see what in me I have to give up to be how I want to be. It has been a painful process and on-going. I have to continue to give up being angry, greedy, a victim, right, controlling, not good enough, afraid, sad, lonely, blaming, and other discovered and undiscovered ways of being that are between me and how I want to be in my life.

I have gone from being an angry, dangerous, explosive, and controlling man to a gentle, compassionate, and loving person. I used to be a very nice guy on the outside hiding a monster inside who protected me from people I thought wanted to hurt me.

I have gone from total denial of who I was to acceptance of who I am. The acceptance of my past and taking responsibility for my life has given me a life, where before I was dead, just a robot figuring out how and what to be, distrustful of everyone including myself.

Life has changed, not only for me, but for my mom, my father, my brothers and sisters, my nieces, nephews, aunts, and uncles, my neighbors and co-workers, my community, and the world. I changed, and the world changed... I went from sucking the life out of my loved ones to giving life to everyone I meet.

I wish I could say that I magically transformed my life into being perfect. The truth is, I am still completely parts of the past. It is an on-going process, not something or someplace that I used to be.

This is who I am today:

- I do what I say when I say I will, and when I realize I have not, I clean it up.
- I keep giving up being right, and I am getting faster and faster at getting off it.
- I am not forceful. I am straight and take what I get.
- I acknowledge my fear and then choose to act.
- I keep giving up "something is wrong here."
- I keep giving up trying to get somewhere, and I accept where I am.
- I share myself with others with a commitment to make a difference for others.

I used to be self-defended. Now I am self-defined. I used to focus on the past and future. Now I live in the present and rely on current information. I used to be controlled by what I thought were obligations and compliance. Now I make choices about my life within the limits I set for myself.

I used to ignore my body and my breathing. Now I am centered in my body, and I am aware of my breathing. I used to be rigid and frozen. Now I am flexible and alive. I used to be disengaged, always playing roles and keeping myself hidden from others. Now I have meaningful contact with others, and I am open and willing to be known. I used to keep myself constantly in control. Now I allow myself to be revealed and vulnerable.

I used to communicate through monologue, rules, and edicts. Now I use dialogue. There is nothing that can't be solved through discussion.

I am living with a new definition of life and ways of being in the world. Life is now a mystery to be lived, not a problem to be solved...

For most of my life, I thought my life sucked and that I had been sentenced to hell on earth. But during the twenty-year journey, I have been blessed in finding my way from the abyss into the sanctuary of love. When I think about my past, I am humbled, grateful, empathetic, touched, moved, and hopeful.

I have a life that was unimaginable just a few years ago. I have learned that I am responsible for 100% of how I respond or react to the world. That is real power, the kind of power that changes lives.

When I started the journey into discovering myself, I was sure I was the victim of a cruel joke. Slowly over the years I have spent less time in that frame of mind and more in the state of mind that I am responsible, even that I am creating my reality. I tried for a very long time to use power to have control over the world or over myself. Simply accepting how I am and that I create how I am with my choices is real power, even though it looks more like surrender.

Life was never the way I envisioned it to be. I created expectations of how it was supposed to look or be, and when it did not appear that way to me, I got upset and blamed someone or something else for my disappointment.

Now I am aware that I have the power to create my expectations. The world is what it is, and I create my response to it. It is not about what I am doing, it is about how I am being with what I have created.

The future for me is happening today. I am happier, safer, and committed to live an inspired life. What does that say? All my life I was committed to surviving. Now today I am committed to contributing to the lives of the people in my world and on this planet. I now have the ability to create any future I desire. Right now I am committed to telling my story in a way that moves people to take action in their own lives and free themselves from the prison of violence and control. My life lacked love, now it is full. So the future I am living into is a future overflowing with love.

I had sought comfort all my life, and in seeking comfort, I denied feeling risk. I was always avoiding feelings I did not like and chasing ones I liked. I was constantly running from something rather than to something. The change was to stop running and just sit where I was and accept it. It was to get very honest with myself about where I was and then seek help to change what was wrong. It was a difficult process, and often I felt desperate, overwhelmed, and sick. I would be able to let go for a minute or two, and then I would grab hold of control again. Even now, I accept that I feel scared, uncomfortable, and at risk or in danger. I make it all right to feel what I feel and then trust myself to know what to do to take care of myself.

As a child growing up, all relationships were based on me being guarded and protecting the secret that I was inherently bad. Now I am able to open myself, and I value every relationship in my life, even from the past. I have a friendship with my first wife and her daughter. I love Sheila and Jennifer. I listen to them and have an interest in their world.

The near-death experience gave me the opportunity to know the difference between being in control and just being. The pancreatic attack was what it took for me to reach a new level in my humanity that I could not reach with control. It was the answer to my prayers. It gave me what I wished for most in life, and it was what it took for me to break up the powerful control I had on my life. What I ask for I will get, what I speak is what I create. Until then, I never believed I had choice. Now I am accountable for my life, and that is very different from controlling.

What does it feel like? It is as though all my life I was holding my breath. I never knew what it was like to take a breath without feeling that I was suffocating. I never knew anything different. It was normal for me to take shallow breaths, always struggling to breathe, thinking that everyone struggles for air. All of a sudden, I experienced taking deeper breaths of air and being more available to life. What was once a very restricted world now seems open and welcoming, even inviting.

I have learned that commitment, hard work, and persistence are not enough. A willingness to let go and accept that things are the way they are, and the way they are not, has incredible power. There are all kinds of therapists, healers, methods, and results, but the bottom line is that it is all up to me, not anyone else.

For me it is a constant process of letting go and letting go and letting go. I have been working at letting go for twenty years and find that there is always something else to let go of. Healing comes from inside, and there is NOTHING, absolutely nothing, that changing the outside accomplishes.

I have found that my wealth is in how I relate to everyone in the world. I am committed to living a life of love, freedom, and acceptance.

I have done my homework from the Hoffman Institute, to love and accept my parents unconditionally. That became my mission, and it is complete.

I have contacted my brother Al and ended the war I had declared on him from birth. My brother Eddie and I have started talking on a regular basis. Jenny is a great friend, and we talk every week. My baby sister, Dee, and I are the best of friends.

The summer after my recovery, I decided to reach out to my father's sister, Aunt Alice. She and Uncle Stan lived in Iowa and would be driving right through Bozeman that July. They agreed to stop for a short visit. We were all instant friends. The following summer, Mom, Jenny, Sheila, Aunt Alice, and Uncle Stan would traveled across Iowa, with Jenny, Stan, and me all on bicycles. Stan was 72 years old at the time.

In August, 2002, one year after I returned to work, I suddenly got an emergency phone call from Jennifer. She said that she wanted to visit and that her mom would have her at a café in Challis, Idaho, the next day at noon. My mom was visiting, and she went with me to pick up Jennifer.

We arrived at the café early, and Jennifer was an hour and a half late. Her mom pulled up behind my truck, Jennifer took her bag from the back seat, and Jane sped off in the direction she had come from. I hugged Jennifer, and she got in the truck. I asked if she wanted anything to eat or drink. We stopped at a gas station and picked up a couple of soda pops.

The first fifteen minutes of the trip were totally silent. Suddenly, Jennifer said, "I'm not going back to my mom's."

After a moment, I said, "Okay, you are not going back to your mom's."

Jennifer was quick to speak. "My mom didn't want me to visit you, and we had a big fight because I wanted to see you."

In the rearview mirror I could see she was crying. "I'm sorry that you and your mom fight," I said slowly.

Jennifer started talking very fast. "My mom was going to kill herself on the way up here. She stopped the car twice and walked down to the river. Then she said she was going to kill both of us by driving into the river unless I promised to go back after the visit. She took my cd's out of my pack. She said they weren't mine."

By this time I had pulled the truck over to the side of the road and was holding her in my arms. She continued to cry and tell me how mad her mom was at her and how she did not want to return to Idaho. She described trying to stop her mom from driving the car into the river and how scared she was. She talked about having to leave her dog and four cats. She cried and cried. Eventually she settled down, and I began driving. Jennifer continued talking about how sick her mom had been and that she would not be able to care for the animals. She talked about how Jane's husband had left. The drive home was almost seven hours, and Jennifer talked the entire way, telling how she had registered for the classes she wanted and now would have to take what she could get in Bozeman. She was really mad about losing her friends and not going to a school she loved. My mom and I listened to Jennifer, and I assured her that she would not have to return to Idaho, unless she chose to do so.

Jennifer's unexpected arrival again in our lives was welcomed by both Sheila and me with full support. She picked out a bedroom in the new house and started making plans for decorating and school. Jennifer had to accept courses that were available, and it was a big price for her to pay for choosing to live in Montana.

Because I've accepted responsibility for my life, I am able to offer my daughter a safe and supportive place to live and grow. I have broken the family curse.

The curse only existed in people's minds. It was an attempt to find meaning when bad things happened. I thought I was a victim of life and everything life did to me, and I was filled with anger. That was the curse. Now I know I have a choice. When I see anger, I recognize that there is some unresolved feeling that I must release, and I set out to recognize, own, and release it. It is now mine, and the anger melts away. Now I see that the challenges in my life have given me a tremendous gift. Nothing was wrong or right. It was just the way it was. The curse was lifted when I took responsibility for my life. And because I am able to share my way of living with Jennifer, she will be free of the curse as well.

In November, 2002, I took an advanced class with Landmark Education. As I sat there in my chair, the forum leader spoke about how human it is to make up stories about why life is the way it is. I agreed, but had no idea of what he was really talking about.

Then he asked me to consider the idea that the war with my brother Al was just my story. I was upset. He then asked me to look at when I first knew my brother was a jerk. My mind flashed through all the things he had done to me: beaten me up, taken my furniture, hit me in the head with a rock when I was seven, teased me about being fat, beaten me up when I was 21 and then again when I was 26. I had lots of evidence of his being a jerk. The entire family supported me in my belief. All of a sudden I knew that he had been this way all his life. I remembered my parents bringing him home from the hospital. In that moment, my world had changed. I was no longer the center of attention, and I knew he was the cause of it.

The next morning, I picked up the phone and called my mom. I asked her for Al's phone number. I had only seen him twice in the past twenty-five years. Our relationship was a war zone. I had never been comfortable talking to him. I made the call and told him I knew now that I had made up that he was a jerk. I asked for his forgiveness for believing all his life that he was doing something to me, when in reality what I was doing was making him wrong. We agreed to get together and start a new relationship.

We moved into our new house in November. In December, my mom mentioned how nice it would be to have all her children together for Christmas, and I flew to Las Vegas to spend the holidays with my family. My sisters and I connected at a level I had never expected. One evening, Dee's husband Bill got drunk, and we brought him home with us. The next morning at 5:00 am, while fighting with Dee, he punched her in the eye. When I found this out, I asked Mom to take the kids to McDonald's while we, my two sisters, Bill, and I, had a talk about what had happened. In the end, Bill and Dee agreed to get counseling and to report to Jenny and me the results.

It is my belief that when a man is violent, the woman must leave immediately and never go back. To him she is like alcohol to an alcoholic. It starts with cursing and name calling, escalates into shoving, and ends in hitting. It is not about her, but he will think it is, and she will, too. There is only one thing to do. Get out immediately.

It is essential to leave someone who is violent because he doesn't know what is driving him and will not stop to figure it out until enough people stand up to him and tell him the truth: "this is not acceptable and you have to leave or I will." It was being left alone with the fear of jail that finally forced me to face myself and make the decision to change.

I wish there were a magic healing factory, but there is not. A person has to decide that he will give anything, absolutely anything including his life, to change.

I justified my acceptance of Dee and Bill's plan to work it out because I had a sense of how Dee could drive anyone crazy, and they have two beautiful children.

The sad thing is, they went to counseling a couple of times, then moved to the east coast. Their five-year-old had problems at school because the fighting had woken him. On advice from the teacher, they talked about what he had experienced, but then it was put away like anything else. Out of sight, out of mind. I talked to my counselor about what I could do. His advice was just to be available to my sister when she needs it, otherwise let it go. It has to be a problem for her before she will do anything.

The following February, I started a seven-month Leadership Course from Landmark Education. In May, my mom arrived for her annual visit. As we were walking one day, I noticed she was having difficulty, and I asked if her hip was bothering her. "It really doesn't bother me," she said. "It's just a little stiff after riding on the plane."

Thanks to the Landmark Forum, my listening was different. I heard what was behind what Mom was saying. I heard fear in her voice.

We completed our walk, and she went to the living room to read. I went downstairs to my computer. I wrote an email to my brothers and sisters sharing what I had seen and heard in Mom's voice. I sought their advice and comments.

I immediately went back upstairs and sat down on the floor at my mom's feet. I started by saying how I was afraid to say what was on my mind and asked if she would indulge the concerns I was feeling. I spilled my guts. I was worried about her hip and wanted to know more about what was happening for her. In listening to her, I learned that she hated hospitals and the pain in her hip was much more than she ever shared with anyone. I heard all the things she had done to avoid dealing with it for thirty years.

I asked, "If I can get an appointment with an orthopedic surgeon this week while you are here, will you go with me?" True to form, she agreed.

"You will never get an appointment. It takes months," she tagged on the end. I smiled as I walked away.

We met with one of the finest orthopedic surgeons in town on Wednesday at noon. That August, my mom had full replacement hip surgery. I went to every appointment with her and was beside her every minute. I joined my wife in being Mom's caregiver. It was the most amazing, challenging experience I have ever had in my life. The doctor said my mom's hip was the worst he had ever seen. Today she is active and pain free.

This kind of care and relationship had never been a possibility in my life before. Until I got that I was the creator of my life, my life was very limited. I only looked at what was safe in relationships, instead of moving past my own fears to the kind of love and caring I wanted in my life.

At Christmastime, I visited with my father. It had been twenty-six years since we had a conversation. He lives alone in his little trailer and seems content with who he is.

I talked my sister Jenny into going with me to visit him. We began a nice conversation, mostly him and Jenny visiting about when we were kids. He seemed to be fine with our visit. I finally asked him what in his life he valued the most of anything. He thought for a few moments and said, "This is not what you might think, but I have valued my right to choose where I go, what I do, and how I think." I was quiet after that. My mind could not wrap around what he had said, but I knew it was a piece of the puzzle of understanding him. Now, looking back, I see that he valued his right to be right and never be wrong.

The next day, I called him and asked if I could come by and visit again. I arrived at his trailer shortly after 4:00 in the afternoon. In the back of the trailer he has a double bed with his TV sitting on a shelf. He took off his boots, and I noted that they were very similar to the ones he had worn all his life, black cowboy-type boots. I also noted the lift inside the right one. He laid down across the head of the bed, and I sat at the foot. We visited about my business ventures, and he did not listen to what I was saying. He kept telling me how I should do things in business, how to deal with partners, how to market. He never heard how successful I was with my life. I am 49 years old and fully retired. I have a fabulous life. But no matter what I said, he continued to talk about the stock market and things that he seemed to enjoy.

After half an hour of listening to him go on and on, I interrupted and said, "I have a question."

He asked what.

"Dad," I said, "I have been trying to clean up messes from my past, and with all the dealing we've had over the years, I am wondering if I owe you anything?" Instantly, his face lit up, and I recognized the look. Things were about to become very dangerous. He appeared so angry that he could barely speak. The words were slow coming out of his mouth.

"Yes," he said. "You owe me $140. You promised to pay me and then had the balls to send me a bad check. You fucked your own daddy. There are over a million people in this town, and I would rather spend time with any one of them than you. You are dumb, really dumb. You are dumber than a box of rocks. If you were on fire, I wouldn't cross the street to piss on you to put it out. You are the last person I ever want to spend time with. You are the worst kind of cocksucker there is. You don't get that the world would be better off without you."

Shock is the only term that could describe my response. "I got that," I said as I stood up. "I've got to go. I have to be somewhere for dinner." His silence threw me. He got up from the bed and stood there looking at me. I repeated, "I have to go." He looked at me and halfway reached out his hand and said, "Well, next time you're in Vegas..."

I could not believe his words. I said, "Merry Christmas," and made my way to the door. I quickly drove away. For three weeks afterwards I was in a daze.

I understand now that there is nothing I can do to ever get him to see me the way I want to be seen. I would still like his approval. I accept that that is in me, but I try not to act on it any longer. I acknowledge his right to his life his way. There is a warm love and compassion in my heart for him. He reminds me of a dog who has been beaten. I never know what will set him off, but I know to keep my distance. And I am committed to giving him love.

Recently, Sheila and I were traveling to visit a friend a hundred miles away. It was a beautiful day, and we were talking about our upcoming raft trip. Sheila was excited about spending five days on a river. She loves fishing and the outdoors. She said, "I'm bringing some flour and bacon for cooking those little Brookies in." Catching fish and eating them is not exciting to me. I remembered my friends saying the only fish you can keep are a certain size.

I said, "They'll have to be the right size."

She fired back, "I'll read all the fishing rules before we go." We sat in silence. My mind raced with how to get Sheila to see that what I had said was innocent.

After ten minutes of silence, I asked, "Is your heart open to me?"

"No," she answered quickly. We rode along another ten minutes in silence, my mind sorting and sorting through what had happened.

Finally, I asked, "Can I share what is going on for me?"

"Sure," she said.

I spoke slowly with the intent to share my deepest truth about what was happening for me. "I'm sorry I upset you. I was only repeating what I heard my friends say the other day. It was innocent. I really was not making you wrong."

Her words were like pouring gas on a campfire. "You were making me wrong," she said.

Something clicked in my mind. "Let me out of this truck," I said. There was anger and determination in my voice. She started to slow down. We were already exiting the freeway and almost to the bottom of the off ramp. "Let me out of this fucking truck now." My words were loud and forceful. I repeated them again. Before the truck came to a full stop, I stepped out. Sheila drove to the bottom of the off ramp and parked the truck. It was maybe a hundred and fifty feet for me to walk.

I went to the driver's window and said, "I am innocent. I did not intend to make you wrong." I was firm that this was a bottom line for me. I must be vindicated.

She looked at me and said, "I have to pee, so get in the truck, and we'll settle this later."

I snottily saluted her and said, "Yes, Ma'am." I walked around the truck and got in the passenger's side.

It was only a couple of blocks to Linda's house. We arrived in silence. We greeted Linda, and I asked her to point me in the direction of her computer. Our reason for visiting was so I could help her set up her computer to get e-mail. I went right to work, and in 30 minutes it was complete. Sheila and Linda joined me at the dining room table. I was feeling sick to my stomach, and my head was aching. I trembled as I started to speak. "I have to talk about something. Will you listen?"

They both looked at me and nodded.

"Something happened this morning on the way over here that really scared me." The words were coming from deep inside me. "I experienced the same rage that destroyed my life in the past. In the past, it has resulted in someone being hurt or something getting broken." I hesitated and continued, "I had hoped I would never see this side of me again. I cannot believe how close to the surface it was. It's the same monster that came out and destroyed my life."

I sat silent for a minute before continuing, "Sheila, I am sorry. I thought I had dealt with all my demons. What I can tell you is that I have counseling tomorrow, and will work through this."

Sheila smiled and said, "I know you will."

"Yes, I will. That you can count on."

Linda said, "Would you like to visit my Buddha and walk around the yard?"

"Not right now," I replied. "I just want to sit here until I feel a little more stable. Maybe in a few minutes."

We walked, visited, and had lunch, and Sheila and I headed for home. There was a distance between us, but I knew that everything would be all right.

After all my work, the rage is still a part of me. It is hard-wired, and I accept that it is there. I have learned the warning signs and how to take care of myself and how to get help. I won't go back to a life that is controlled by fear and where fear is allowed to turn into anger and destruction. I have a better life now, one of love and joy and meaning. It is a continual letting go, and it is worth it. I will be strong, have courage, and know that I am the creator of my experience. I will create ripples of love in the hearts of all whom I shall meet.

Everyone asks, "What changed you?" There is not an answer. It is an on-going process. The other day at lunch I saw my first counselor from twenty years ago. I remember her saying it is like the unpeeling of an onion. You can peel off the outer layers of the surface and go back to living. Or you can spend years looking for the essence of your being. The choice is yours. Since then I have had many "life altering" experiences. Each time I make adjustments to my behavior, my thoughts, my environment, or my actions. It all helps. I have found that I continue returning to being a victim of life. I experience being powerless, frightened, and alone. I pick up my favorite defensive tool, anger, and then I gently set it down. I remember the family slogan, "It is not his fault. He didn't mean to do it." Every time I choose being defensive, the experience is the same. I lose the magnificence of life to a world of destruction and anguish. Then I surrender, my breath returns, and love thrives inside me.

Balance in life is a moment to moment movement, not something you get and keep, or can take for granted. Balance is the center we all dance around. I am learning to dance with my fellow humans, and now that I have the basic steps, it is just practice, practice, practice...

Farewell

It is a cold, windy winter night in January, 1959. I have just turned six. I am getting ready for bed. My father is yelling at my mom in the other room. Today I went to church with Grandma and learned about praying to God. As I crawl between the cold sheets of my bed, I pull my teddy bear close and start repeating over and over and over, "God, please help me."